Hear Our Voices!

Engaging in Partnerships that Honor Families

Bweikia Foster Steen

National Association for the Education of Young Children
Washington, DC

National Association for the Education of Young Children

1401 H Street NW, Suite 600
Washington, DC 20005
202-232-8777 • 800-424-2460
NAEYC.org

NAEYC Books

Senior Director, Publishing & Content Development
Susan Friedman

Director, Books
Dana Battaglia

Senior Editor
Holly Bohart

Editor II
Rossella Procopio

Senior Creative Design Manager
Charity Coleman

Senior Creative Design Specialist
Gillian Frank

Publishing Business Operations Manager
Francine Markowitz

Through its publications program, the National Association for the Education of Young Children (NAEYC) provides a forum for discussion of major issues and ideas in the early childhood field, with the hope of provoking thought and promoting professional growth. The views expressed or implied in this book are not necessarily those of the Association.

We would like to thank our funder for their generous support for NAEYC equity initiatives, including the development of this book.

Permissions

NAEYC accepts requests for limited use of our copyrighted material. For permission to reprint, adapt, translate, or otherwise reuse and repurpose content from this publication, review our guidelines at NAEYC.org/resources/permissions.

Figure 5.2 on page 102 is adapted from a visualization created by Gina Tomko and *Education Week*, informed by Ruby Nadler, PhD, leadership consultant; SIGMA Assessment Systems, Inc.; and *Education Week* reporting, for A.M. Bichu, "7 Ways School Leaders Can Master Nonverbal Communication," *Education Week* (September/October 2022).

Photo and Illustration Credits

Copyright © Getty Images: cover (all), vi, 4, 28, 47, 50, 70, 85, 88, and 97 (all)

Illustrations by NAEYC: 21, 100, and 102

Library of Congress Control Number: 2022943553

ISBN: 978-1-952331-18-3

Item: 1166

Contents

About the Author

Bweikia Foster Steen, EdD, is associate professor and internship coordinator in the early childhood education program in the College of Education and Human Development at George Mason University. She received her doctoral degree from the University of San Francisco in international and multicultural education. Dr. Steen has over 25 years of experience in early childhood education. Previously, she taught children from birth through age 8 in the San Francisco Bay Area and on the collegiate level at California State University, East Bay; New York University; and Trinity Washington University. Her research focuses on promoting social, emotional, and academic success among children of color during the early years and providing early childhood educators with developmentally appropriate practices and strategies that will enable this success.

Acknowledgments

I want to thank my mom, Acquainetta Street, my first and most important teacher and advocate, for always using her voice to ensure my hopes, dreams, and goals were achieved. To the families who fearlessly shared their stories and trusted me to share their stories in turn, thank you! Your voices are heard and valued. I thank Rossella Procopio, Dana Battaglia, and NAEYC for believing in this work, for assisting me throughout the process, and for their commitment to diversity and equity. I am grateful to Stephanie Calabrese for devoting time to assisting with research. To my family and friends, thank you for your continued support and encouragement. To my daughters, I will forever share your stories and advocate for you. Your tenacity and resilience inspire me!

Hear Our Voices! Engaging in Partnerships that Honor Families

Introduction

This book emphasizes the importance of working with young children and their families in order to meet the social, emotional, and academic needs of all children through reciprocal family partnerships. "Educators who engage in developmentally appropriate practice take responsibility for forming and maintaining strong relationships with families and communities" (NAEYC 2020, 18). The relationship among child development theories, developmentally appropriate practice, anti-bias education, and a strengths-based approach is discussed, as well as how they all contribute to positive, effective collaboration. Above all, this resource illustrates the significant contribution families can make to the education of their children when their voices are heard and included.

How This Book Is Organized

This book includes five chapters.

Chapter 1: Why Family Voices and Their Stories Matter digs into why it is important to listen to families, discusses the author's own research on the topic, and presents an overview of the role child development theory and research plays in forming reciprocal family partnerships. Understanding the impact families have on their children's development and learning is a critical first step to partnership.

Chapter 2: Building Reciprocal Family Partnerships takes a deeper dive into explaining what a reciprocal family partnership is and how it works.

Chapter 3: Creating a Caring Community and Welcoming Environment discusses the *why* and *how* of creating a positive culture and climate that honor all families, both in the classroom and more broadly throughout the early learning program.

Chapter 4: Meeting the Needs of Families Through Assessment examines the purposes of assessment and the various types of assessments commonly used within early childhood settings. It also explores the significant role families play within the assessment process.

The first four chapters also include the following features:

> **Guiding Questions,** at the beginning of each chapter, invite readers to consider what they already know about key concepts that will be explored.

> **Family Voices** features the real words of families that the author has dialogued with in her research. This feature appears at the beginning of and embedded throughout each chapter in connection with key concepts being explored. (*Note:* To keep the authentic voices of these families intact, editing was kept to a minimum, but names have been excluded or changed to mask identities. In many cases, some contextual information about the quoted family member's ethnicity and household is included. These details are provided to show the range of diverse families represented.)

> **Reflect,** at the end of each chapter, asks questions that prompt readers to think back on the key concepts and consider how those ideas might apply to their own practice.

> **NAEYC Standards** from the "NAEYC Early Learning Program Accreditation Standards and Assessment Items" and the "Professional Standards and Competencies for Early Childhood Educators" are also highlighted at the end of each chapter.

Finally, **Chapter 5: Strategies and Activities for Honoring and Partnering with Families** summarizes key points from the first four chapters and offers concrete strategies and activities that teachers and school leaders can implement to promote reciprocal family partnerships.

CHAPTER 1

Why Family Voices and Their Stories Matter

Guiding Questions

As you read this chapter, consider the following:

1. What's your story?

2. What has been your path to becoming an educator?

3. What was your family's role in your schooling?

4. What drives your desire to collaborate and work with young children, families, and the early learning program's community?

FAMILY VOICES

One of the things that I think can happen among administrators and teachers, and bridging that gap and building a healthy relationship with the parents, I think is first, we've got to feel like we're being heard. When I'm up there and I am coming to you with my concerns, I want to feel like you hear me—that what I'm saying is being considered, and you're trying to figure out what we can do to make this better. I want to be heard.

—Black mother in a single-parent family with a 5-year-old child

---

Each child who enters an early childhood program or classroom has a family and a story. *Family* is defined in different ways for different people. Children's relationships with family members, their family configuration, their family's socioeconomic status, and their cultural background and context are just some of the factors that affect their unique path of emotional and cognitive development (Fields, Meritt, & Fields 2018). When educators understand these factors and how they impact children's development and learning, they can better meet the needs of both children and their families. Educators' work with children and families is based on foundational studies and research. Research-based knowledge helps educators appreciate the role families play in their children's development and learning. It also helps them gain an understanding of their own beliefs and biases related to family partnerships and how these can affect their work with families. Adapting educational philosophies and approaches to match the realities of the families you serve is critical to your work. Part of that work is getting to know each child and family, which requires intentionality, empathy, and understanding.

This chapter introduces my (the author's) journey as an early childhood educator learning from and collaborating with families, and it further explains why educators must provide the space, time, and opportunities to listen, learn, and reflect. My journey toward having intentional partnerships with each family was not automatic. It developed through a process of time, reflection, research, and experiences that shaped my beliefs on the important role of partnerships between early learning programs and families. It stemmed from conversations with families who insisted that I engage them in their children's learning, families who required that I view partnerships through a different lens, and families who told me what I was doing wrong and why they didn't feel comfortable completing certain activities I sent home.

Understanding Family

Koralek, Nemeth, and Ramsey (2019) define *family* as "one or more children and the adults who have sole or shared primary responsibility for the children's well-being as the children's guardian and primary caregivers" (6). These authors expand on this definition by stating that "family can include adults who are the child's biological or adoptive parents, other close family members, or other individuals such as foster families and guardians who are committed to supporting the child emotionally, financially, or both. Family members may live in the same household or in different households" (Koralek, Nemeth, & Ramsey 2019, 6–8). By broadening the idea of who and what makes up a family, educators recognize that they will engage with diverse family structures, including, but certainly not limited to, families with same sex parents, heterosexual parents, a single parent, unmarried parents, and grandparents as primary guardians (Granata 2014; Koralek, Nemeth, & Ramsey 2019).

Likewise, educators will encounter diverse cultures, languages, traditions, beliefs, and behaviors that are passed down from one generation to another (Hammond 2015). Holidays, foods, types of dress, and daily routines may be different from one child or family to the next. Each of these contexts influence and inform whole child development and learning. The diversity families bring into the school setting provides context for collaboration, partnerships, and learning from one another. Engaging in these partnerships helps families feel respected, welcomed, and valued, and children feel safe and affirmed in an inclusive environment.

Why Family Voices Matter

Families are children's first teachers. Educators who acknowledge and understand this simple statement know that a dialogue about children begins with their families, and they respect the voices and perspectives of the families as collaborators in the development of the children. Paulo Freire, a Brazilian educator and philosopher, stated that "education is dialogue" and "the process of dialogue demonstrates that there is no fixed outcome, that all involved (including the teacher) are open to new ideas and insights, and are willing to review, reflect on, and change their ideas" (Veugelers 2017, 414). Unfortunately, not all families are welcomed or feel a connection to their child's early learning program or educators.

For example, as a first year teacher, my primary contact with families was during family-educator conferences, which occurred in November and March. During each conference, I would review the child's report card and ask the family if they had questions. With this approach, I was unintentionally separating home and school. I believed that I was partnering with each family by sharing their child's report card and my goals for the child; instead, I was telling the family what was going to happen. A better strategy would have been to involve and engage the family by asking about their experiences as well as the strategies they use with their child. Then, we could have collaborated in decision making and goal setting.

Recognizing that the voices of those who have been silenced are powerful is the important first step of meeting the developmental and learning needs of the whole child. This belief recognizes that a family has ownership over how best to support their child and acknowledges that without their partnership, fundamental insight into the individual development and identity of their child is missing. Through open and honest dialogue, all stakeholders work to build an understanding of an issue without the pressure to make decisions or be right. It opens the door for all parties to express ideas, desires, and expectations (Graybill & Easton 2015). True dialogue has the ability to link investigation, reflection, and action to change. Through dialogue and intentional active listening, stories are shared, experiences are valued, and connections are made. By actively listening to the children and families' voices and stories, educators learn about the diverse contexts, stories, cultures, languages, and experiences each brings into the school and classroom environment. Active listening requires engagement, curiosity, and understanding. Educators listen to learn, and then they take what they have learned and build from it. In this way, educators start to build relationships with families, which ultimately lead to partnerships.

Throughout this book, you will read excerpts from authentic dialogues with families presented in the recurring "Family Voices" feature. Each dialogue raises the voice of one or more families. Some contextual information about each family is provided to illustrate their diversity. Although each story is unique, there are common threads that run through all of them that help to provide context for what families need from educators.

Creating a school and classroom space where all voices are heard and included requires suspending judgment; being open and receptive to learning, unlearning, and relearning; and having an unwavering commitment to equity and inclusion for all families. *Inclusion* is feeling safe, engaged, respected, and valued. Families need to know that their voices matter and will be intentionally included. They need to know that their opinions, beliefs, concerns, and ideas are valid, appreciated, received, and acted upon. Intentionally including diverse families' voices means transforming the early learning program's environment, processes, and policies versus expecting families and children to conform to traditional school expectations. "Through our stories, we call attention to racism and discrimination and assert our fundamental human dignity" (Proctor 2021, n.p.). This means committing to adopting a mindset that values reflection, checking for implicit bias, and recognizing the strengths each family brings to the early learning program setting.

Equity is the relentless focus on eliminating inequities and increasing success for all groups by identifying who benefits from and who is burdened by and left out of schoolwide decisions (Nelson & Brooks 2015). Across all roles and settings, advancing equity requires dedication to self-reflection, willingness to respectfully listen to others' perspectives without interruption or defensiveness, and commitment to continuous learning to improve practice. "Members of groups that have historically enjoyed advantages must be willing to recognize the often-unintended consequences of ignorance, action, and inaction and how they may contribute to perpetuating existing systems of privilege" (NAEYC 2019, 5). To counter institutional exclusionary practices that have impacted the perceptions of some families, including families of color and families with children with disabilities, teachers and school leaders must invite, include, and listen to the voices of those who have been silenced or ignored. These families must be viewed as equal partners who share the same goals and can help forge the pathway to accomplishing those goals.

Applying an equitable and reciprocal family partnership philosophy means understanding that meeting the whole child's developmental and learning needs requires taking full accountability for initiating collaboration with each child's family. Henderson and colleagues (2007) outline eight fears that may prevent educators from partnering with families, of which I highlight four:

> **Fear of being called racist or insensitive.** Continuously reflect on your biases and learn more about anti-bias education. Don't be afraid to ask friends, colleagues, and families about outreach practices you want to use to receive feedback.

> **Worry about losing power and control.** The goal of a reciprocal family partnership is to empower the families.

> **Low confidence in families' knowledge and judgment.** Families enter schools and classrooms with a vast amount of knowledge, experience, and talent. Capitalize on their expertise.

> **Breaking away from safe and traditional types of family involvement.** The first step is to get started and try. Start by making a phone call, sending a video of the child completing a lesson, or sharing a laugh with a friend. Whatever you do, *start*.

Distrust, Victimization, and Trauma

The early childhood education field must move beyond equating *family involvement* and *family partnerships* as synonymous. The difference between the two is that family involvement practices have the tendency to leave some families feeling powerless and unimportant in regards to their child's education. Too often, educators leave marginalized families out of the decisions that directly impact their children's learning and development. These families are told what is going to happen, sent information about interventions that will occur, or asked to attend a meeting where they are expected to listen but not provide input. Likewise, school- and classroom-initiated family training workshops have the potential to perpetuate structural inequities built on prejudices and assumptions about families. Ultimately, school-initiated family training workshops leave some families feeling as though their voices are shut out or left out of the conversation. In addition, they may have witnessed school- and classroom-based practices and microaggressions that sent a perceived message that their voices, beliefs, and services are not wanted or valued. This all leads to families feeling distrustful of the school, victimized, or even traumatized.

Trauma is defined broadly as an experience or event that is a threat to yourself or someone close to you. Trauma comes in many forms, and it is not only the event itself but the response to the stressful situation and the undermining of the person's ability to manage that response (Erdman & Colker with Winter 2020). According to the National Child Traumatic Stress Network (NCTSN; n.d.), "some groups of children and families are disproportionately represented among those experiencing trauma. This means that they may be exposed to trauma at particularly high rates or be at increased risk for repeated victimization" (n.p.). Families who experience institutional and structural inequities may develop a distrust of and a sense of isolation in the school system. In other words, even during the early years of schooling, as early as prekindergarten and kindergarten, these families may have learned through experiences with their child's school that the school system may not have their child's or family's best interest in mind. As research demonstrates about the impact of trauma, these experiences manifest as one of the three main types of traumatic stress reactions: re-experiencing (thinking about the trauma), avoidance (staying away from people, places, and/or activities because these reminders are upsetting), or the fight-or-flight response (NCTSN, n.d.). These behaviors are often viewed by school leaders and teachers as signs that families are uninvolved with, argumentative about, or unresponsive to their children's schooling. In reality, families are responding to a type of trauma they hold that's rooted in their past experiences with an inequitable school system.

Countering this narrative "requires attention to both *interpersonal* dynamics—the day-to-day relationships and interactions at the core of early childhood education practice—and *systemic* influences—the uneven distribution of power and privilege inherent in public and private systems nationwide, including early childhood education" (NAEYC 2019, 4). To promote equitable school-based inclusivity for all families, teachers and school leaders should intentionally evaluate school systems and policies that adversely influence their perceptions and practices, which could place barriers between families and their children's school and classroom programs.

Three Keys to Reciprocal Family Partnerships

To help minimize the stress or anxiety families might feel when working with you, consider the following tips. These are values of trauma-informed care (Meeker 2015), but they can apply more broadly to any reciprocal family partnership (Erdman & Colker with Winter 2020, 77):

1. Ensure that when families meet with you, they feel physically and emotionally safe.

2. Be transparent and trustworthy.

3. Share decision-making responsibilities with family members.

Anti-Bias Education and Families

Early childhood educators should understand the role that anti-bias education plays in dedicating themselves "to self-reflection, a willingness to respectfully listen to others' perspectives without interruption or defensiveness, and a commitment to continuous learning to improve practice" (NAEYC 2019, 5) that is underlined by knowledge about developmentally appropriate practice, which recognizes the individually, culturally, linguistically, and ability appropriate goals for each child. In this approach, educators work to bring together knowledge about child development theories and anti-bias education to inform decisions that will promote equitable opportunities for engagement and partnership for all families.

Anti-bias education is a "commitment to supporting children who live in a highly diverse and yet still inequitable world," and it "is based on the understanding that children are individuals with their own personalities and temperaments and with social group identities based on the families who birth and raise them and the way society views who they are" (Derman-Sparks & Edwards with Goins 2020, 4). An anti-bias education approach asks educators to reflect upon the biases and beliefs that place barriers before individual families instead of honoring and supporting them (Hill, Newton, & Williams 2017). All educators enter their classrooms with their own norms, biases, and expectations. These norms are based on home experiences, cultures, and personal and professional experiences with the early learning program environment. They often lead to expectations about the knowledge a family should have about school as well as expectations about a family's level of engagement with their child's school and the classroom. However, an educator's own norms and beliefs can impede on their ability to intentionally develop positive relationships with each child's family to understand their wants, needs, concerns, and experiences and to capitalize on what they do versus what they don't do (Trivette & Keilty 2017). Furthermore, an educator's lack of cultural awareness can lead to untrue assumptions and negative outcomes for a child and their family (Kostelnik et al. 2019). An anti-bias educator is committed to reflecting on biases to ensure equitable opportunities for each child and their family. Embracing an anti-bias education approach "acknowledges that everyone has lived their lives in a system that is racist; that we all come with and act on biases, especially when unchecked or monitored; and that we are inundated with images and messages that influence how we think about and respond to one another" (Allen et al. 2021, 50–51). Educators must reflect on their own norms and beliefs as they strive to gain a better understanding of other norms and beliefs and partner with each child's family to better serve that child.

Anti-bias education provides four core goals for educators:

> **Adult Goal 1, Identity:** Increase your awareness and understanding of your own individual and social identity in its many facets (race, ethnicity, gender, ability, sexual orientation, family structure, economic class) and your own cultural contexts, both in your childhood and currently.

> **Adult Goal 2, Diversity:** Examine what you have learned about differences, connection, and what you enjoy or fear across all aspects of human diversity.

Adult Goal 3, Justice: Identify how you have been advantaged or disadvantaged by the isms (ableism, classism, heterosexism, racism, sexism) and the stereotypes and prejudices you have absorbed about yourself or others.

Adult Goal 4, Activism: Explore your ideas, feelings, and experiences of social justice activism. Open up dialogue with colleagues and families about all these goals. Develop the courage and commitment to model for young children that you stand for fairness and to be an activist voice for children. (Derman-Sparks & Edwards with Goins 2020, 19)

My Work with Families

It's clear that all voices are not being heard. I decided to start listening. For over two decades, I have dialogued with over one hundred families, including linguistically and culturally diverse families, families from one- and two-parent households, adoptive families, military families, families from low-income households, and families of children with special needs. I conducted these dialogues using participatory action research, a methodology with the objective of handing power from the researcher to research participants, drawing on the experiences of the participants, and giving voice to the ones whose voices are often not heard or included in the discussion (Mammen et al. 2019).

Our conversations were loosely structured around the following questions:

1. What are your thoughts related to reciprocal family partnerships? How would you define reciprocal family partnerships?

2. What strategies does your child's school use to establish reciprocal family partnerships?

3. What characteristics do you desire from your child's teacher(s)? How have those characteristics helped to cultivate relationships and partnerships?

4. What characteristics do you desire from your child's administrator(s)? How have those characteristics helped to cultivate relationships and partnerships among all families?

5. What strategies do you suggest administrators and teachers use to promote partnerships among families with children who are culturally, linguistically, and ability diverse?

6. What are some ways you think teachers and administrators can partner with diverse families to better serve those families and the community?

7. How do school settings embark on a journey of ensuring reciprocal family partnership through dialogue?

During the dialogues, families shared their goals and dreams for their children and how their children's teachers, school leaders, and early learning programs could partner with them. Through these dialogues, stories were told about families who were eagerly welcomed into their child's school, families who were not welcomed, families who felt as if they belonged in a school community, and families who felt as if they were negatively labeled from the first

Voices of Families

Last year was rough because my granddaughter had teachers who did not understand her creative side, and they weren't concerned that she was already gifted and talented. She was bored in the classroom, and even now she's a bit bored with the reading level that they have her on. We're always pushing for more, but they want her to stay back to read with her class.

We have made several suggestions to the teacher to up her reading level and that she goes to a different classroom for reading. In her previous school, when she was in first grade, she read with the third graders. At this school, they would not allow her to read at a different level. They keep her, like I said, behind her reading level. We're having to, at home, push her and encourage her to read at her own level. We want the teacher to challenge her a little bit more. We don't want him to be offended by it and take it out on her.

—Black grandmother in a family with a third grade child

• • • • • •

What isn't working is the strategies they have for my son. They are not proactive; they're more reactive, even though they know that he has a tendency to get excited and use his body or get frustrated and bite because he is not too verbal yet. He is developmentally appropriate for where he should be at his age, but since there are kids that are in his class that have stronger communication skills, I think that's probably another reason why he's a little bit more frustrated with himself, so he is acting out by using biting or hitting or slapping. He can comprehend and absorb everything around him, he just isn't able to verbalize yet how he is feeling.

I think for us, it is the way that they keep communicating to me that there's always something wrong. Being a teacher, I know how important it is to phrase what you say to parents in a productive manner instead of all of these problems that are happening and not being proactive. All of the solutions that I've put in place for my son have come from strategies I've learned from the resources at my school or just being a teacher and understanding child development and strategies that have to be put in place. He is a very gentle child, but he's got a lot of energy, and all of his reactions usually come from being overstimulated and he is usually happy. It's not an anger situation. I just want better communication. I want some more positive feedback. I don't want to just hear negative, and I also want to know what led up to the situation.

—White mother in a two-parent family with a 2-year-old child day of school. What would often start out as a scheduled 30-minute conversation would end up taking hours because families simply needed someone who listened to their concerns, reflected upon them, worked with them to create solutions, and reassured them about their advocacy efforts. Families wanted teachers and school leaders who were willing to take the time to build trust, develop a teamwork philosophy, and dedicate time to learn about the uniqueness of each child and their family. They desired a school community that would be willing to acquire knowledge about each family and use that knowledge to build positive and reciprocal partnerships. Ultimately, families needed a trusting educator who would unwaveringly stand alongside them as they navigated this process we call *school*.

It's important to put yourself in the families' place to understand their expectations:

> **Talk with me.** Ask, "What do you need, want, and expect from your child's school?" Remember to provide communication in the various languages represented within the school community. Stand at the school's front doors during drop-off and pickup, greeting families and engaging in dialogue that helps school leaders craft communication that is transparent and that promotes collaboration (Graybill & Easton 2015).

> **Welcome me.** All families need to know that they are a welcomed, valued member of the school environment. Families want to know that they are part of a team composed of school directors and administrators, teachers, staff, and families who will put their child's strengths, interests, and needs first. Placing pictures of families in the entrance; sharing instruments, dance, and traditional clothing; and putting displays in the hall to showcase cultures are examples of things schools may choose to demonstrate support and an inclusive environment.

> **Listen to my ideas.** Acquiring intentional and thoughtful knowledge related to the families served affords school leaders, teachers, and staff the opportunity to better understand the vital role families play in young children's lives. This knowledge helps inform educational policies and practices related to family engagement and to developing trusting reciprocal partnerships. Educators must seek various approaches to acquire knowledge that will foster a deeper awareness of the factors and the influences, such as cultural background, funds of knowledge, and family configuration, that impact development and learning. This will assist with better understanding the strategies needed to appropriately meet the needs of the children and their families by adapting philosophies that match the realities of the families served.

In my research, I have learned that families who felt connected with the early learning program and their child's teachers experienced ongoing opportunities of respect, belongingness, and inclusion. They experienced school leaders and teachers who were relentless in their commitment to partnering with each child's family by setting aside judgment in their attempt to connect. "To nurture a relationship into a partnership requires intentional time and effort" (NAEYC 2022, 145).

Supporting Children Who Are Gender Expansive

Signe (White mother in a two-parent family with three children, one of whom is gender expansive): One of the incidences was around Christmas. The kids were making gingerbreads in school. We don't celebrate Christmas, but that's not the point in this instance. My kid's kindergarten teacher said, "If you're a girl, put the bow on the head, and if you're a boy, put it on the neck." My child was like, "They're just paper gingerbread. Why? I want to put it on the neck." The teacher just reiterated what she had previously said. My child looked to the assistant teacher, and she was like, "Well, can I put the bow where I want to put it?" The assistant teacher said something a little more supportive, but not enough that then my child actually put it there. She did end up putting it on the head. It was one of those things that they hang outside the classroom. By the time it came home in January, she had ripped the bow off.

Bweikia Steen: What did she say was her reason for ripping the bow off?

Signe: She ripped it off the head and tried to stick it on the neck where she wanted to put it. She's the kid who will raise her hand. I always say to her when you raise your hand and you speak up, it's awesome because you're speaking up for yourself. There might have been another kid in that class who for whatever reason wanted to put the bow on the belly button. Want to have two bows or whatever, right? So, I reached out to that teacher, and I just said, "Here's what happened." I said, "To her and to me, it felt like a microaggression the fact that she couldn't put that where she wanted." Her teacher is Indian. I said I imagine that these may be experiences in other contexts that you might have had. I don't even know if I said that I said something like "I'm sure you can understand" or something like that. She was like, "Oh my gosh, I totally get it. Thank you." It was like she hadn't clicked. Maybe we went back and forth a little bit more. Although I don't know if she went back and talked to my child about it.

In first grade, my child had an absolutely amazing teacher, who unfortunately is no longer at the school. She was so awesome, and that was the COVID year too, so she didn't even get her the full year. She was the teacher who when my child brought in the book *A House for Everyone*, which goes through all different ways of expressing and identifying in terms of gender, she read the whole thing. I said to my kid, "Did she read all the pages?" She read all the pages; she talked to the kids. Because I reached out to her and I said, "My child is bringing in a book with a lot of big ideas. She's really adamant that she wants to share it with you and hopes to share it with her friends. Let me know if you want to chat about it." She didn't really. She's like, it fits perfectly in with what we're talking about anyhow. I don't know if that was true or not, but she worked it out. She did it as a read-aloud and gave my child the opportunity to say I love this book because I'm just like Ivy in this book. Her teacher was like why are you like Ivy? My child didn't talk about the gender. She said, "Because I'm a really fast runner like Ivy is, and I have short hair like Ivy." It helped her friends too to see other right representation. There were a lot of other instances throughout the year, and we communicated a lot. In fact, she's somebody who I'd actually like to write an article with because we have lots of emails back and forth about really supporting my child in this developmental time too because this was before, when she was like, "Oh, it's okay if somebody calls me a boy."

What Families Want

Regardless of family background or configuration, home language, or experiences, all the families I spoke with had much in common when it came to their hopes and expectations for how educators would engage with them while navigating their children's education. These commonalities, which go hand-in-hand with guidelines and recommendations from NAEYC's "Developmentally Appropriate Practice" (2020) and "Advancing Equity in Early Childhood Education" (2019) position statements, have been distilled into three points that represent what families want and value most, and they serve as the focal points explored in this book:

1. **Reciprocal Family-Educator and Family-School Partnerships**

   Supported by

   - "Developmentally Appropriate Practice" position statement: "Educators acknowledge a family's choices and goals for their child and respond with sensitivity and respect to those preferences and concerns. Gather information about the hopes and expectations families have for their children's behavior, learning, and development so that you can support their goals" (NAEYC 2020, 18).

   - "Advancing Equity in Early Childhood Education" position statement: "Be curious, making time to learn about the families with whom you work" (NAEYC 2019, 8).

   - "Developmentally Appropriate Practice" position statement: "Actively engage family members and the broader community in all aspects of program planning and implementation, recognizing and taking into account the systemic inequities that can make it difficult for members of traditionally marginalized groups to participate" (NAEYC 2020, 30).

   - "Advancing Equity in Early Childhood Education" position statement: "Create meaningful, ongoing opportunities for multiple voices with diverse perspectives to engage in leadership and decision making" (NAEYC 2019, 9).

2. **A Caring and Welcoming Environment**

   Supported by

   - "Developmentally Appropriate Practice" position statement: "Educators welcome family members in the setting and create multiple opportunities for family participation" (NAEYC 2020, 18).

   - "Advancing Equity in Early Childhood Education" position statement: "Maintain consistently high expectations for family involvement, being open to multiple and varied forms of engagement and providing intentional and responsive supports" (NAEYC 2019, 8).

3. **Assessments That Meet Families' Needs**

   Supported by

   - "Developmentally Appropriate Practice" position statement: "The methods of assessment are responsive to the current developmental accomplishments, language(s), and experiences of young children. They recognize individual variation in learners and allow children to demonstrate their competencies in different ways" (NAEYC 2020, 20).

   - "Advancing Equity in Early Childhood Education" position statement: "Use authentic assessments that seek to identify children's strengths and provide a well-rounded picture of development" (NAEYC 2019, 8).

Using knowledge about child development as well as developmentally appropriate practice, a strengths-based approach, and anti-bias education to inform your reciprocal family partnership practices demonstrates a commitment to diversity, inclusion, and equity. Through these professional teaching practices, families can feel safe and reassured, trusting that the school and classroom climate, the curriculum, and instructional and assessment practices are implemented in an equitable manner that appropriately embraces each child's funds of knowledge. "Building on the strengths and assets and using them to make connections to new learning help create robust, welcoming, and meaningful early learning experiences for all children" (NAEYC 2022, 57). Ultimately, a family wants to feel confident that their young child is in a safe school and classroom environment where their culture, beliefs, and experiences are valued and their individual, developmental, and learning needs are met. Each chapter will provide developmentally, individually, culturally, and linguistically appropriate examples and strategies that emphasize and are grounded in anti-bias education and a strengths-based approach that school leaders and teachers can easily implement to promote reciprocal family partnerships.

Developmentally Appropriate Practice

Developmentally appropriate practice refers to applying knowledge of child development, individual development, and cultural and linguistic assets in making well-informed, intentional school and classroom decisions. It promotes supporting and scaffolding every child's development and learning with approaches that are strengths based (which is discussed later in this chapter and in more detail in Chapter 2), play based, joyful, and engaging (NAEYC 2020).

> The nature of children's skills and abilities, experiences, languages (including dialects), and cultures is likely to vary greatly within any single group of young children and over time. Early childhood educators must have an extensive repertoire of skills and a dynamic knowledge base to make decisions, sometimes balancing what at first appear to be contradictory demands, in order to address this wide range of diversity. (NAEYC 2020, 34)

Each child's and family's funds of knowledge must be respected and integrated within the early childhood setting. *Funds of knowledge* are defined as the bodies of knowledge, including information, skills, and strategies, which underlie household functioning, development, and well-being (Moll et al. 1992). Funds of knowledge include the knowledge, experiences, and expertise each family brings because of their culture, community, traditions, and routines (Moll et al. 1992). Capitalizing on each child's and their family's funds of knowledge recognizes and builds on the strengths and the knowledges they have. Seeking and learning about each family's funds of knowledge helps develop connections and relationships and demonstrates to families a willingness to understand how each of the child's contexts is interconnected and important to their development. For example, conducting home visits is one way to learn about each child and their family's funds of knowledge and use that information to make connections among the home and school. As discussed later in the chapter, Bronfenbrenner's theory, too, "underscores the importance of considering the multiple contexts and illustrates how the child's interactions within all of these systems affects the child's growth and development" (NAEYC 2022, 62). This knowledge about how people learn within their cultures and contexts is also reflected on to build successful reciprocal family partnerships. Without knowledge about child development (based on research), individual development (based on personal observations and information shared by the children's family), cultural development, and linguistic development (based research and on funds of knowledge), educators make assumptions that can lead to barriers in children's development, achievement, and engagement. Being grounded in this knowledge base helps educators to avoid "fall[ing] back on making decisions based on vague notions that are part personal values, part memories, part expediency, and part images of desirable future behavior" (Gestwicki 2017, 7).

I know the importance of understanding families and using their funds of knowledge. In particular, I experienced the perils of not doing so, especially when discussing the assessment process and making informed decisions about young children because of my own experience as a parent navigating the school system with a child with a disability. For instance, my daughter was diagnosed with an articulation delay at 3 years old. She aligned with the learning progressions that children typically follow across most development domains (i.e., physical, cognitive, social and emotional); however, while her receptive language skills were developing as expected, her expressive language skills were not. Because of this articulation delay, it would be easy for an educator to assume that she was delayed in all developmental domains. However, an intentional educator would understand the role of developmentally and individually appropriate expectations, use ongoing developmentally appropriate assessments to determine strengths and areas of need within each domain, and balance those findings with the knowledge gained through ongoing dialogues with the child's family about the speech services the child was receiving to inform teaching decisions and practices moving forward. Therefore, such as in the case of my daughter, engaging a child's family in the assessment process provides invaluable information to appropriately meet a child's individual developmental and learning needs.

Consider the following guidelines for developmentally appropriate practice (NAEYC 2022) and how each applies to reciprocal family partnerships—not just the guideline that explicitly mentions these partnerships:

1. **Creating a caring, equitable community of learners.** This includes partnering with children's families, welcoming them as important members of this community who bring valuable knowledge and skills that must be appreciated and integrated into the early

learning program setting. A community of learners includes the child; teachers; school leaders; staff members; peers; and community members characterized by relationships, safety, inclusion, and a positive school climate.

2. **Engaging in reciprocal partnerships with families and fostering community connections.** This is done by intentionally establishing reciprocal family partnerships as the heart of the early learning program's mission and vision. Reciprocity is accomplished through strategic, intentional, and ongoing dialogue; through exchange of resources, knowledge, and information; and through collaboration.

3. **Observing, documenting, and assessing children's development and learning.** This is done by including all key stakeholders within the assessment and decision-making process: families, children, teachers, school leaders, specialists, and related community members. Intentional assessment ensures that families are knowledgeable about the purpose of the assessment, the data collection and analysis process, and how to interpret the results to co-create goals and decisions. At the same time, stakeholders partner with the child's family to co-create and determine best strategies to provide ongoing support.

4. **Teaching to enhance each child's development and learning.** This is done by using the funds of knowledge of each child and their family and by conducting ongoing, anti-bias, strengths-based observations and assessments (seeing what a child can do versus what they can't do) to inform instructional and curricular decision making that promotes success for each child in all learning domains.

5. **Planning and implementing an engaging curriculum to achieve meaningful goals.** This is characterized by engagement, collaboration, and cohesion among school leaders, teachers, staff, families, and children to consider each child's developmental, individual, cultural, linguistic, and ability needs.

6. **Demonstrating professionalism as an early childhood educator.** This is an intentional focus on ethical and professional dispositions through self-assessment and reflection of biases, assumptions, and practices. It is an ongoing process that involves a willingness to listen, learn, and collaborate with all key stakeholders through honest dialogue that leads to action and advocacy for and with young children and their families.

Child Development Theory and Research

Note: The following discussion is not intended to provide extensive information. Instead, it demonstrates the role that knowledge pertaining to child development plays in informing beliefs and practices related to reciprocal family partnerships. It touches on a number of broad points to inform and promote reflection on your own reciprocal family partnership philosophy in an effort to understand how reciprocal family partnerships should work in the ever-evolving world of education.

Research demonstrates time and again that families play an important role in their children's social, emotional, and cognitive development, which ultimately helps to shape and inform the children's identities. Children whose families are actively involved in their education are more likely to succeed socially, emotionally, and academically (Barger et al. 2019; Smith et al.

2019). This is because "during the early years, the brain matures faster than at any other time of life, and brain development is shaped by genetics and the child's environment" (Bassett et al. 2018, 2).

The early childhood years, birth to age 8, represent an important time in child development. During these years, many factors influence a child's identity development, including their family makeup and economic situation; their personal identity, culture, language, and religion; and their community, school, teachers, and peers. According to the National Council for the Social Studies (2010), "personal identity is shaped by an individual's culture, by groups, by institutional influences, and by lived experiences shared with people inside and outside the individual's own culture throughout her or his development" (17). In other words, children do not leave their culture, identity, and experiences at the front door before entering the school building. The different aspects of a child's life are interdependent with one another and work together to influence the child's behavior, temperament, attitude, and engagement in school. Understanding this requires an intentional belief that families are their children's first teachers; thus, they play a salient role in their child's developmental outcomes. Research in early childhood education has shown that educators who embrace a child's family as essential and fundamental to the child's development and learning more intentionally use this knowledge to cofacilitate learning and development for each child (Epstein & Sheldon 2006; Lin & Bates 2010). Although educators must critically examine various child development theories for bias and relevance to the population and the school and community demographics they serve, they must also reflect on specific theories and philosophies that illustrate the important role families play in promoting positive child development and learning outcomes that help educators to adapt and individualize daily decisions.

The Background/Framework

Acquiring knowledge on child development theory informs the practices that influence decision making related to young children and their families. Knowledge of research theory and practice is essential to becoming an intentional teacher who builds partnerships with and supports families (NAEYC 2022). Although the latest research debates total reliance on theories that privilege some while leaving out others, ultimately the theories adopted by educators support educational practices and decisions (Karpov 2014). Let's take a look at one theory that is particularly relevant to building reciprocal family partnerships.

Philosopher Urie Bronfenbrenner's ecological systems theory laid the foundation for recognizing the importance of the relationships, interactions, and interconnectedness among the child's environments on whole child development and learning. Bronfenbrenner's ecological approach focuses on the holistic nature of human development and explains how a child's different contexts and environments work together to influence and impact the child (Hayes, O'Toole, & Halpenny 2017). In other words, this theory suggests that the different contexts are interrelated among the multiple spheres of ecological frameworks (i.e., systems), thus influencing the way children live, develop, and learn (Bronfenbrenner 2005). The many influences on a child's life impact development and learning; consequently, educators must form partnerships with families to gain insight into these influences to meet the needs of the child.

The ecology of human development involves scientific study of the progressive, mutual accommodation throughout the life course, between an active, growing human being and the changing properties of the immediate setting in which the developing person lives as this process is affected by relations between these settings and by the larger context in which the settings are embedded. (Bronfenbrenner 1989, 188)

While there are five systems (see Figure 1.1 on page 21), let's focus on the first four systems and how each context impacts and influences young children's development: microsystem, mesosystem, exosystem, and macrosystem.

The *microsystem* is the closest and the most immediate context to the child. The microsystem includes aspects that influence the child's daily life, such as interactions with their family members, teachers, and peer groups. In Bronfenbrenner's theory, families are important and viewed as providing significant influences on children's development (Rosa & Tudge 2013).

Equally important, the next layer is the *mesosystem*. This layer is a system of two or more microsystems. For example, the child connects the experiences acquired from their family to those acquired while in school. The relationships and experiences from the child's home (with family members) and school (with educators) play a role in development and learning, demonstrating the importance of intentionally building reciprocal relational opportunities among all contexts (Eriksson, Ghazinour, & Hammarstrom 2018).

The *exosystem* includes the external environmental settings, which indirectly affect development. This system can include family income and work commitments. For example, a family member that works three jobs may not have time to volunteer in the school or attend family-educator conferences; furthermore, the stressors associated with working three jobs may impact the child's behavior at school and in the classroom (Bronfenbrenner 1979). The exosystem can impact a child's behavior at school even though the child may not directly interact with these contexts. When children are aware that their family members aren't available to attend activities at school, it does have an effect on them. For example, during a schoolwide family breakfast, the child whose parents are not able to attend because they are working might display signs of withdrawal, loneliness, and sadness, thus impacting development and behavior.

Finally, the *macrosystem* includes the child's cultural patterns and values as well as political, societal, and economic systems and values. Passed-down cultural values and beliefs influence the decisions the family makes, including school-related decisions. Approaches, attitudes, and behaviors related to school and classroom involvement and engagement may also be passed down from generation to generation based on past experiences. When a family witnesses the adult members attending school functions, they are more likely to do the same as it becomes a part of their culture. Thus, the macrosystem plays a role in family involvement and engagement (Bronfenbrenner 1979).

Figure 1.1. Bronfenbrenner's Ecological Systems Theory

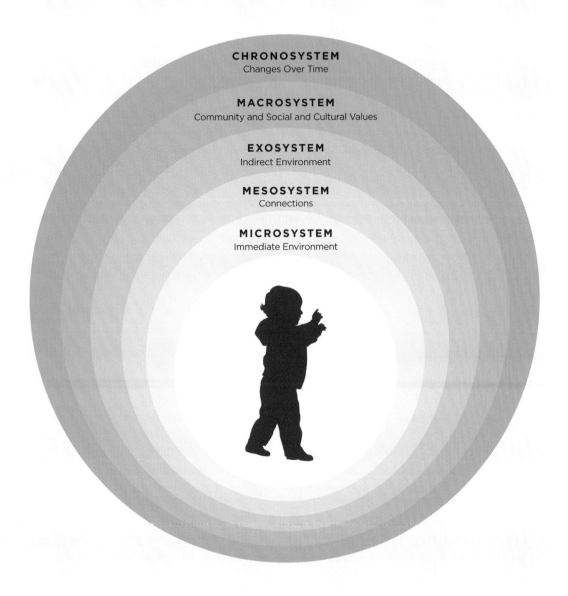

The five systems of Bronfenbrenner's theory.

Let's draw on the first two key elements of Bronfenbrenner's model—microsystem and mesosystem, which are the two systems of more immediate connections to the child—and reflect on reciprocal family partnership practices. Both the microsystem and the mesosystem shape and influence young children's lives. Bronfenbrenner focused attention on the importance of the dynamic relationship and interdependence between individuals and the broader contexts in which they are situated over time. In the early childhood setting, the child's home and school environments matter, and thus, the child actively and constantly attempts to make connections and seeks to find relevance between the two to adapt understanding. The development of the child depends on the existence and the construction of understanding of the interconnections between the settings and environments, reinforcing the importance of bridging the connection between home and school (Gray & MacBlain 2015). "This includes joining participation, communication, and the existence of information in each setting about the other" (Bronfenbrenner 1979, 7), which has significant implications for guiding, developing, and implementing reciprocal family partnerships. In a reciprocal family partnership, it is understood that child development occurs from the many influences on the child, the child's world, their family, their school, their experiences, and their exposures.

"If we want to understand the person and the person's unique development, we have to understand their ecosystem" (Shelton 2019, 13). Consequently, the child's total interactions combine to nourish and encourage healthy development and learning. The microsystem (family, school, peers), mesosystem (religious affiliations, neighborhood, workplace), exosystem (economic systems, political systems, education system, government system), and macrosystem (overarching beliefs and values) shape and influence the child's learning and development.

Foundational Theory and Current Context

"There is growing awareness of the limitations of child development theories and research based primarily on a normative perspective of White, middle-class children without disabilities educated in predominantly English-language schools" (NAEYC 2019, 6). An awareness of the ongoing changes within the early childhood field is imperative because the child's interactions at home, in school, with peers, with their culture, and in various environments are influential and essential to positive development and learning (Bronfenbrenner 2005).

> While some research-based norms provide guidance regarding healthy child development and appropriate educational activities and expectations, these norms have too often been derived through research that has only or primarily included nonrepresentative samples of children or has been conducted primarily by nonrepresentative researchers. Additional research, by a more representative selection of researchers and theorists, is needed to develop new norms that will support equitably educating all children. (NAEYC 2019, 18)

Therefore, it is critical to place this theory within the context of current practice and research. Bronfenbrenner adds to the body of developmental knowledge that directly informs understanding and practices related to child development and family influence. Moreover, NAEYC (2019) posits that early educators must "recognize that the professional knowledge base is changing" (6).

Table 1.1. Bronfenbrenner's Theory into Practice

Ecological system	Brief definition	Concrete strategies
Microsystem	Most immediate context to the child; includes aspects of the child's daily life, such as interactions with family members, friends, teachers, and neighbors	• Intentionally initiate relationships with each child's family • Invite families into the school and the classroom • Conduct home visits • Conduct community walks to gain a better understanding about the school community and the community where the children live • Engage families in an individualized family questionnaire or video introductions as one way to learn about each family • Provide families with daily videos or pictures of their children
Mesosystem	Connections between two or more microsystems, or immediate environments, such as the home, school, or neighborhood	• Bridge the home-school connection by conducting home visits • Involve families in shared decision making about the classroom or school environment and individualized instructional practices • Provide varied options and opportunities for families to share about their culture, religion, language, or favorite hobby (e.g., in-person or video conference visits, prerecorded videos, home artifacts) • Attend community and school events that families attend
Exosystem	External environmental settings that indirectly affect a child's development, such as the family's income and workplace	• Use the knowledge acquired from families to reflect on each of the family experiences and circumstances, how they impact the child, and the practices that will counter the barriers that might prevent development and learning • Document what you know about each child and their family • Conduct biweekly or monthly check-in calls, emails, postcards text messages to provide information about the child's progress and discuss individualized action plans
Macrosystem	Includes the child's cultural patterns and values as well as political, societal, and economic systems and values (e.g., laws and regulations)	• Take the time to learn about each child's culture, identity, experiences, and interests • Embrace the child's culture and family values by providing a mirror and a window through children's books, family guest speakers, pictures, and videos • Provide varied opportunities to openly dialogue with families about school values versus societal values versus home expectations (e.g., home visits, back-to-school nights, monthly check-in sessions)

Each context must be appreciated and incorporated throughout the school and classroom experiences to recognize and honor the importance of multiple influences that shape, guide, and inform children's growth and development (NAEYC 2022). Doing so ensures young children can make connections between their home and school contexts. By drawing on children's preexisting knowledge, teachers can scaffold and enrich children's understanding of new ideas and skills learned in school. Furthermore, these factors help to conceptualize practices that will provide "equitable opportunities to those who have historically or are currently being marginalized from experiencing high-quality early learning" (Alanís & Iruka with Friedman 2021, 19). Keeping each child's contexts in mind also capitalizes on the "funds of knowledge that children and families bring as members of their cultures and communities" (NAEYC 2019, 7). In other words, young children bring the knowledge, culture, and experiences gained from their home with them when they enter school; thus, it is important to capitalize and integrate their funds of knowledge into all aspects of the school and classroom climate. "Children's interests are stimulated by the experiences they engage in with their families, communities, and cultures" (Hedges, Cullen, & Jordan 2011, 187).

The child's interactions at home, in school, with peers, with their culture, and in various environments are essential to the child's development and learning (Bronfenbrenner 2005). These total experiences help to shape the child. According to Shelton (2019), "the essence of facilitating development is to create environments, relationships, or activities that support and enhance the child's understanding of the world and ability to function in it" (12). Bronfenbrenner's model demonstrates the diverse influences and needs of young children and the importance of being aware of, understanding, appreciating, and including the child's contexts to support the child's development. In early childhood, this can be accomplished through the use activities that involve and engage the child's microsystem, thus partnering to ensure the microsystem and mesosystem are interconnected. Each child and family is unique, belonging to multiple social and cultural groups. "Each has dignity and value and is equally worthy of respect. Embracing and including multiple perspectives as a result of diverse lived experiences is valuable and enriching for all" (NAEYC 2019, 13).

As theory is applied to practice, one important piece to consider is how to effectively involve and engage the actual stakeholders and participants: children's families. Child development theories identify and include the child's family as experts in their child's learning. But how do educators ensure that the voices of all families are heard, included, and engaged in practice?

In my first year of teaching in the San Francisco Bay Area, I was the teacher who reached out to all families, but I must admit that I gravitated to the ones who challenged me with ideas and suggestions and to the ones who were available to volunteer. I understood the importance of involving and engaging families and had learned about theorists such as Bronfenbrenner in my early childhood courses, but it was easier to partner with the families who were actively pursuing me. During this time, I had a dialogue with a Spanish-speaking mother who changed my approach and beliefs on finding encouraging ways to partner with all families. One morning, she dropped her first grade child off inside my classroom instead of at the front office. She asked me about her child's progress. Mayelin, the first-grader, translated for her mother. I invited the mother into the classroom, where she shared that she would like to spend time in Mayelin's classroom but had a 9-month-old daughter and no child care. She also shared that she was nervous to speak in public because of limited English. She didn't know if she had anything to offer to the class. I reassured the mother that she would be an asset in our class, and we would work together to ensure Mayelin's developmental and academic success. After confirming with my school principal, I invited the mother to come into the classroom whenever she was available and to bring her 9-month-old with her. The smile on her face told me a lot. In the beginning, Mayelin's mother would quietly observe from a seat in the back of the room. Eventually, she and her 9-month-old baby dropped Mayelin off at my classroom door more frequently. I started to look for her and was always happy to see her. We would engage in conversation; the more I engaged her in conversation and developed a relationship, the more time she spent in my classroom. As the year progressed, the baby would join the class during circle time on the rug and the mother began sharing her culture during class time. Before long, she even overcame her fear of speaking in public and would teach the class Spanish. Mayelin had a very successful year of development and learning, and I gained a partner.

This initial conversation with Mayelin's mother gave me a better understanding of the importance of consistent reflection on my own biases. I needed to intentionally initiate and nurture reciprocal family partnerships with all families. This mother felt comfortable enough to express her desire to partner with me and was willing to reveal her fears. Biases based "on race, class, culture, gender, sexual orientation, ability and disability, language, national origin, indigenous heritage, religion, and other identities are rooted in our nation's social, political, economic, and educational structures" (NAEYC 2019, 4). I learned to embrace the fact that the families who seemed more reserved, more distant, or less interested also had a story; they had hopes, dreams, and goals for their children. Furthermore, they had history, experiences, culture, and languages that influenced their children's development. I realized I could learn more from each family if I was willing to embrace their different parenting styles. I repositioned my stance on family partnerships to build a safe and trusting environment where I deliberately partnered with all families. By the end of the year, my partnership with Mayelin's mother had grown beyond expectation. She had reformatted my family website and family newsletter to ensure it was an interactive, two-way communication newsletter (see Chapter 2), and she also started a Spanish-speaking family club, which initially began with the families in my classroom and later expanded to the entire school. School leaders and teachers have the ability to activate the social capital within families who have otherwise been silenced (Charania 2021). When they take the time to acknowledge families' funds of knowledge and build trust by fully listening to them, families will share their stories, their skills and knowledge, their wants, and their needs.

Summary

Early childhood educators cannot teach a child without a clear understanding of child development and a respect for each child's funds of knowledge, culture, languages, and experiences that they bring into the classroom. NAEYC (2020) states that "each child is a member of family, community, and cultural groups that shape the child's development and learning from birth" (14). Individualizing expectations, interactions, involvement, and engagement will ensure that a child's needs are being serviced. Equally important is differentiating partnership expectations and involving and engaging all families within the school and classroom experiences so young children and their families can make and see connections between home and school.

Bronfenbrenner's theory demonstrates that the home plays an integral role in development and that both home and school play a role in a child's development and identity. Therefore, it is imperative that both parties work together to support the total developmental needs of the child. Educators must ensure that all families have a voice within the school and the classroom. This is accomplished by intentionally creating "meaningful, ongoing opportunities for multiple voices with diverse perspectives to engage in leadership and decision making. Recognize that implicit biases have often resulted in limited opportunities for members of marginalized groups. Consider and address factors that create barriers to diversified participation (e.g., time of meetings, location of meetings, languages in which meetings are conducted)" (NAEYC 2019, 9). Becoming familiar with and using the child development educational theories and models such as a strengths-based approach and anti-bias education informs the practices and philosophies educators adopt within school and classroom settings.

Reflect

1. Think about the guiding questions posed at the beginning of the chapter. Reflect on the family stories in the chapter. How do they compare with yours? How does your role as an educator make you think about your own family's stories?

2. What are your funds of knowledge? In other words, what skills, talents, expertise, cultures, and languages do you bring to your school and classroom setting? How do you use them to connect with the families you serve?

3. What is your understanding of anti-bias education? What questions do you have? How might you explore this further?

4. What is the connection between child development theories and family engagement? How do they support each other? How does one inform the other?

This chapter supports the following:

NAEYC Early Learning Program Accreditation Standards and Topic Areas

Standard 7: Families

7.A Knowing and Understanding the Program's Families

7.C Nurturing Families as Advocates for Their Children

Professional Standards and Competencies for Early Childhood Educators

Standard 1: Child Development and Learning in Context

1c: Understand the ways that child development and the learning process occur in multiple contexts, including family, culture, language, community, and early learning setting, as well as in a larger societal context that includes structural inequities.

Hear Our Voices! Engaging in Partnerships that Honor Families

CHAPTER 2

Building Reciprocal Family Partnerships

Guiding Questions

As you read this chapter, consider the following:

1. How would you define *reciprocal family partnerships*?

2. Have you ever had to wait for your talents to be appreciated? How long did it take? What steps did you take to help move the situation along? How did you feel during the waiting process?

> **FAMILY VOICES**
>
> [When] the pandemic hit, my son's teacher always made sure she reached out to make sure he was getting what he needed. I made it very clear when he went into first grade that he's going to be bored out of his mind going to school virtually. We knew that. That was our choice to keep him out because we wanted to make sure that the kids who really needed the teacher's attention got the teacher's attention. My children had me at home with them. I chose not to work so I could give them attention. I checked with the teacher and I said, "Hey, is his reading in the corner during instruction time, is that going to bother you?" She's like, "No, because every time I ask him a question, he is answering them." She was fabulous. I never asked for it, but she made sure he was never bored. She would drop off packets at every child's home. She always made sure to include challenging math items in there for him because she knew he loved math and puzzles.
>
> —Asian mother in a two-parent military family with two children

What early childhood educators believe and the personal experiences they have with their own families and early learning programs inform their interactions, engagement, and mindset related to partnering with the many diverse families they encounter. Although the field understands that families are their children's first teachers and have a prominent role in shaping their children's identities, welcoming and building reciprocal partnerships with all families requires educators to evaluate themselves and the school policies and procedures related to families and the community.

For educators to build reciprocal family partnerships, they must understand what this term means and how such a partnership works. Educators must focus on *reciprocity* in the partnership to make it beneficial for everyone involved, including children, families, and themselves. Educators must listen to and exchange ideas with families, working together toward the success of each and every child. It's not about just sending emails or holding family-educator conferences. The process is more complex and requires deeper thought and commitment.

It is critically important for educators to first examine the root cause of their own biases and assumptions about families and recognize the disparities diverse children and families face within the early learning program. Understanding yourself helps you to understand and relate to others. Think about the families you have served. Did you view any as uninvolved or overly involved in their children's education? What were your perceptions of each type of family? Consistently examining and evaluating your thoughts, opinions, and assumptions helps to address inequitable practices. This allows for co-creation of intentional opportunities for all families that will honor and affirm their identities, cultures, experiences, and expectations.

Most early learning programs have policies and practices for family engagement and outreach. However, if these policies and practices are based on expectations that families will always respond, attend, and engage simply because the school has requested their involvement, they are doomed to fail the families who may benefit the most from more interaction with the school and educators. Families who do not meet these expectations might then be viewed as uninvolved, uninterested, or unable to actively participate in their child's education. Deficit thinking about families can lead to a disconnect between program offerings and families' actual needs and preferences (NAEYC 2022). Acknowledging that there are beliefs, policies, and practices that unconsciously exclude some families is the second step to building reciprocal family partnerships. Educators must continuously engage families in dialogue to listen to their stories, needs, and concerns; learn from them; and reflect on the information gained to inform these beliefs, policies, and practices.

As early childhood educators embark on this journey of self-reflection and evaluation to transform ideas and practices related to reciprocal family partnerships, they must be willing and prepared to listen to and learn from others. This chapter explains reciprocal family partnerships by encouraging educators to reflect on their own biases, listen to key stakeholders, and build on the strengths of each family served. Definitions for the approaches that guide this book (i.e., developmentally appropriate practice, a strengths-based approach, and anti-bias education) will be shared. Partnering with each child's family is an important process teachers must engage in to ensure whole child learning and development. "A partnership implies trust and respect and that those involved are working together toward a common goal or action, such as supporting children's learning" (NAEYC 2022, 145).

How Reciprocal Family Partnerships Work

Reciprocal family partnerships recognize the shared intent and responsibilities of the educator and families to collaborate and to create opportunities for children to develop and learn (Epstein et al. 2019; Sheridan & Kim 2015). They move beyond connecting families to resources or inviting them to preplanned family workshops—which treat families as vessels that must be taught how to help their child—and instead recognize them as their children's first teachers who bring invaluable knowledge, skills, experiences, and resources to the early learning program.

Engaging families in preplanned school activities and family-educator conferences is just a single facet of building relationships and partnerships with families. Educators might wonder, "How do I partner with all families?" The answer is not simple, but it is critically important. Think about the following terms used to describe the process of inviting and including families in their children's development and learning: *family participation, family involvement,* and *family engagement.* While related, these models are not interchangeable. Participation is not the same as involvement, and neither is the same as engagement; furthermore, each is only one component of a reciprocal family partnership.

Family participation. *Family participation* involves educators teaching families skills to work effectively with their children (Knowlton & Mulanax 2001). This approach has the tendency to "normalize particular forms of participation, while ignoring others" (Lowenhaupt 2014, 535). The early learning program or teacher provides the information, and the family receives that information and is expected to abide by and use it to assist the teacher with the child's development and learning. Examples of family participation include back-to-school nights, open houses, content-related family workshops predetermined by the program or educator, volunteering, and family-educator conferences.

Family involvement. *Family involvement* is defined as a "systematic approach which involves supporting, educating, and ensuring family participation in education" (Kuru Cetin & Taskin 2016, 107). Participation is a co-constructed, shared responsibility between families and early learning programs (Weiss et al. 2009). This approach considers how and in what capacity families can be involved in their children's education. However, one of the downsides to solely relying on this approach is that it implies that families listen to, participate in, and implement expectations and requirements set by the early learning program; in other words, it is "often linked with parent education" (Gonzalez-Mena 2007, iv). "Merely *involving* families in their child's education, however, can have the unintended consequences of making parents feel like helpers who follow the teacher's directions rather than equal partners" (Koralek, Nemeth, & Ramsey 2019, 8).

Family engagement. *Family engagement* "is a desire, an expression, and an attempt by parents to have an impact on what actually transpires around their children in schools and on the kinds of human, social, and material resources that are valued within schools" (Barton et al. 2004, 11). The National Association for Family, School, and Community Engagement (NAFSCE; 2022) identifies four main domains representing the core competencies of family engagement:

1. **Reflect** by learning about and honoring the cultural and linguistic diversity of families and communities and exploring with families how children develop, grow, and change.

2. **Connect** with families and communities.

3. **Collaborate** with families around children's learning and development.

4. **Lead** alongside families.

According to NAFSCE, family engagement is collaborative, culturally competent, and focused on improving children's learning. Engagement requires more commitment to shared decision making and empowerment than either participation or involvement (NAFSCE 2022). As Ferlazzo (2011) puts it, "involvement often leads with its mouth—identifying projects, needs, and goals and then telling parents how they can contribute, [. . . while] engagement tends to lead with its ears—listening to what parents think, dream, and worry about" (10).

Examples of high-impact family engagement strategies that NAFSCE offers include (1) building personal relationships, respect, and mutual understanding with families; (2) sharing data with families about children's skill levels; (3) listening to families about their children's interests and challenges and using this information to differentiate instruction; (4) incorporating content from families' home cultures into classroom lessons; and (5) aligning family engagement activities with early learning program improvement goals.

While there are some benefits to these traditional models of inviting and including families in their children's learning and development, they are typically one-sided approaches that fail to give educators the knowledge or insights they need to provide learning experiences that are fully responsive to each child's developmental and learning needs and experiences (NAEYC 2020). Reciprocal family partnerships build on the positive foundations of participation, involvement, and engagement to create ongoing, supportive, and two-way collaboration between educators (both school leaders and teachers) and families. Partnerships are an essential part of the early learning program community and whole child development. *Reciprocity* "generates a momentum of its own that motivates the participants not only to persevere but to engage in progressively more complex patterns of interaction, as in a ping-pong game in which the exchanges tend to become more rapid and intricate as the game proceeds" (Bronfenbrenner 1979, 57). This approach recognizes that families and educators share the responsibility for helping children to develop and learn successfully and make connections among home, school, and the community (Epstein et al. 2019; NASEM 2016). Reciprocal family partnerships acknowledge that three contexts (home, school, and community) work together to promote and support children's learning and development, while upholding that families are the primary context for and the experts on their children's development and learning (NAEYC 2019).

Feeling Welcomed into the School

I think that we—the schools and the families—have to open ourselves up to each other. We have to accept each other with open arms. I think that it should be a partnership, almost like the parents—those who can do it—have to stay at the school on a consistent basis. One thing I did mention is my mother-in-law works at my one son's school. She retired; she was sitting home, didn't do anything. She said, "I need a job." She went to the school just to apply, and so she's like the grandmother of the school. Now, one thing I will say about that is that I get a lot more information and I get a lot more feedback about things that I would not have gotten feedback about because they know that she works there. That's what missing. We're missing those grandmothers, those grandfathers that aren't doing anything. Pull those folks into the schools. Open the schools to the families, so the families can be open to the schools.

—Black father in a blended two-parent family with three children

Developing reciprocal family partnerships that are built on respect, belonging, and trust takes time, communication, and teamwork. Educators take responsibility for initiating dialogues with families, nurturing those relationships, and codeveloping an understanding of what a reciprocal relationship looks like for each family. The two-way nature of reciprocal family partnerships ensures mutual respect and cooperation as everyone works together to achieve shared goals (NAEYC 2020, 2022). It also invalidates the one-size-fits-all approach to inviting and including families in their children's learning and development that treats and expects the same from each family. The emphasis is on doing things together *with* families versus doing things *to* families (Ferlazzo 2011).

Children do not leave their cultures, languages, and home experiences at the early learning program's front doors (Bronfenbrenner 1979). Parenting practices also are influenced by attitudes, which in this context refers to families' perspectives or reactions with respect to the roles and importance of family and parenting in children's development, as well as family members' responsibilities. Attitudes may be part of a set of beliefs shared within a cultural group and founded in common experiences, and they often direct the transformation of knowledge into practice (NASEM 2016). Furthermore, attitudes and behaviors stem from past experiences that shape how individuals perceive their current situations.

Families of color and diverse families have historically been expected to attend school events, reach out to school leaders and teachers, and readily accept the advice and suggestions from educators without being afforded opportunities to provide their own input. They are expected to passively participate—to remain voiceless, silent, and uncomplaining (Carter 2005; Cork 2005; Gonzalez-Mena 2007). This narrative tends to place the blame on the families when the program's expectations related to family relationships and partnerships aren't met. This approach is also based on a single viewpoint centered on dominant groups of people—those who are White, middle class, and have power and privilege.

Five Facts About Reciprocal Family Partnerships

1. All families want to partner with their child's early learning program. They have hopes, goals, and dreams for their child and want to share them with you (Silloway & Szrom 2022).

2. Reflecting on your beliefs and assumptions to determine strategies you can use to demonstrate awareness and appreciation of family members' cultures, identities, experiences, opinions, and input demonstrates an openness to listening to and respecting families. You build trust with families when you value them and seek ideas and opinions from them (Bullard 2017).

3. Creating welcoming school and classroom climates and environments and embracing inclusiveness of all cultures, languages, and experiences promotes the feeling of belongingness. This helps families feel more accepted and supported.

4. Individualizing and using a strengths-based approach to reciprocal family partnerships ensures that families feel safe and cared for and that their cultures, identities, talents, and experiences are validated and honored (Trivette & Keilty 2017).

5. Applying an anti-bias education approach requires reflection and evaluation of personal and professional biases. It requires adjusting mindsets that are based on norms and expectations that do not honor all families. "We must always regard the context in which children and families are embedded, honoring the diversity and dignity of every child and family" (NAEYC 2022, 62).

Reciprocal family partnerships are not based solely on the behaviors and actions of families in early learning programs. They intentionally seek to ensure that each family has a presence within the program by cultivating environments that address threats, microaggressions, and exclusionary practices. Reciprocal family partnerships acknowledge that the level of involvement, participation, and engagement may differ for each family. This approach also respects and values each person's time, efforts, contributions, and commitment. Rather than judging families based on their level of involvement, the focus is cultivating relationships that develop into equitable and reciprocal partnerships. The interactions with, outreach toward, and expectations of the family are intentionally individualized and continuously evaluated to ensure all stakeholders—and the children above all—benefit. "Information about individual children [is] shared by each of the partners [. . . and] each partner contributes specific expertise" (Koralek, Nemeth, & Ramsey 2019, 9).

Table 2.1. One-Sided Family Participation Models Versus Reciprocal Family Partnerships

In one-sided family participation models, educators . . .	Whereas in reciprocal family partnerships, educators . . .
Invite families to preplanned early learning program events	• Invite families to share their wants, needs, goals, desires, and expectations, as well as the ways they would like to and can be involved in planning early learning program events • Ask families which formats and timeframes for meetings and events best meet their needs • Ask families to share their talents and assure families that the knowledge they have is valuable and welcome when shared with the learning community
Set the agenda for family-educator conferences	• Involve families in the family-educator conferences process, including decision making, setting goals and expectations, action steps, and follow up • Provide families with a planning document at the beginning of the school year and ask them to jot down their goals for their child. Educators are clear that they will revisit the document together periodically during the school year and that families may make any changes or additions to the document throughout this time (e.g., creating new goals, sharing strategies that assist with accomplishing those goals).
Create a program or classroom webpage where photos and videos of the children are posted and sent to families weekly	• Invite families to share their ideas and wants related to the content presented through the various forms of communication (e.g., webpage, family newsletter) • Invite families to create content or take ownership of parts of the webpage or family newsletter (e.g., dedicating a section where, on a weekly basis, a different family shares information about themselves with the other families)

Grounded in Anti-Bias Education and a Strengths-Based Approach

Gonzalez-Mena (2007) states that "you can't have a partnership without trust. A partnership implies equity and shared power rather than one side dominating the other" (iii). Intentional educators capitalize on and value the strengths of each family, recognizing families as equal teammates, because they understand that "developmentally appropriate practice requires deep knowledge about each child, including the context within which each child is living" (NAEYC 2020, 18). Furthermore, they regularly examine the biases, attitudes, or stereotypes that favor one group over another. An anti-bias education approach means teachers and school leaders work to build trust with families and children through self-reflection and an understanding of the children and families they serve.

An anti-bias education approach recognizes that inequities stem from systemic injustices and institutional racism, which impact policies and procedures (Derman-Sparks & Edwards with Goins 2020). Historically, families of color, families of children with disabilities, families who speak languages other than the national language, and families who experience socioeconomic insecurity are inundated with systemic educational inequities that have profound developmental and academic effects on their young children (Alanís & Iruka with Friedman 2021; Silloway & Szrom 2022). Family-related educational policies and practices have marginalized, oppressed, and ostracized diverse families because the "educators who shape schools and classroom learning may be unfamiliar with the traditions, assets, and experiences of many of the children and families they serve, and this mismatch can hinder efforts to provide all children with equitable learning opportunities" (NAEYC 2022, 49). Systemic injustices and institutional racism disproportionately impact practices and outcomes for diverse children and their families and place barriers to learning and to acquiring trusting reciprocal family partnerships. According to NAEYC's (2019) position statement on advancing equity, those who have historically been advantaged by the systems of privilege in place need "to recognize the often-unintended consequences of ignorance, action, and inaction and how they may contribute to perpetuating existing systems" (5). In short, reciprocal family partnerships acknowledge the need for school systems to reevaluate current practices that ignore, judge, and silence diverse families.

A Commitment to Anti-Bias Education

A commitment to anti-bias education requires educators to reflect on their conscious and unconscious assumptions, beliefs, values, cultural practices, and experiences to understand how they may influence relationships with children, families, and communities. Assumptions, beliefs, and values might grow to become biases, which can be explicit or implicit. *Explicit biases* are acknowledged, obvious prejudices toward certain groups of people based on their identities, including race, language, economic status, gender, ability, and religious affiliations. This reflection requires a commitment to recognizing that everyone has biases that must be challenged and critiqued. NAEYC (2022) states that "biases include unspoken assumptions about the causes and impacts of children's behavior, developmental progress, identified disability, or academic capability, and can inhibit teachers' ability to understand how their

FAMILY VOICES

Recognizing Each Other as Experts—and Learners

I feel like it's like walking alongside together with humility. Like, sure, I'm the expert in my child because I'm with them all day long and you are an expert in education because you've been trained in that and that's what you do all day long, but we're humble enough to see that in each other. Also, humble enough to say what we don't know, even in our area of expertise.

—White mother in a two-parent family with three children, one of whom is gender expansive

Table 2.2. Questions Versus Dialogue Entry Points with Families

Question	Dialogue Entry Point
Does your child like school?	What does your child say about school? Who do they mention they play with? What is their favorite thing to do at school? What are your thoughts about your child's school and classroom environment?
Did you attend the IEP meeting?	I would like to review the purpose and process of the Individualized Education Program, or IEP. Then, I think it would be helpful to talk about the ways we can work together to accomplish the goals.
How do you want to be involved?	Our school's mission is to partner with each child's family. This year, we will use the Seesaw app. Tomorrow morning, we will stand at the front door to assist you with downloading the app onto your phone and to explain its purpose. If you prefer a different method, please let us know.

context impacts their perceptions" (52). "Most early childhood teachers are sensitive to explicit bias and, for the most part, work hard to avoid and address such behavior" (Derman-Sparks & Edwards with Goins 2020, 10). *Implicit biases* are associated with unconscious perceptions or stereotypes that nonetheless have far-reaching impacts. They create structural barriers, inequitable outcomes, and disparities (DeHaney, Payton, & Washington 2021). Implicit biases reflect an individual's socialization and experiences within broader systemic structures that work to perpetuate existing systems of privilege and oppression (NAEYC 2019), and they manifest through one's actions, words, and thoughts. For example, implicit biases can manifest in the way teachers ask families questions (see the examples in Table 2.2 on this page).

A school leader who has committed to including an anti-bias education approach in the program's mission and vision is committed to reflecting on the role of implicit biases in decision making, embodying an openness to learning from children's families, and acknowledging that families are the heart of the early childhood program to ensure equitable opportunities for learning and development for each child and their family (Alanís & Iruka with Friedman 2021). In programs that put anti-bias education at the forefront, all families are included within the evaluation and reflection process of questioning, exploring, analyzing, and developing solutions. Families need to be able to trust that the program is inclusive, supportive, and validating of their identities, cultures, languages, abilities, interests, and strengths. Together, the program and the families work to understand each stakeholder's role in the development and learning of their child.

Furthermore, in this type of setting, every member of the learning community is recognized as a critical part of developing trust and relationships among diverse families—office staff, custodians, before- and after-school staff, teachers, and school leaders. For instance, greeting each family member as they enter and walk around the school building sends a message that all are a welcome part of the learning community. I have walked hallways where I was greeted by one or more staff members, and I immediately felt welcomed. I have also walked hallways where not one person greeted me.

Looking to NAEYC Position Statements

Reciprocal family partnerships are supported by the

- "Advancing Equity in Early Childhood Education" position statement (NAEYC 2019)
    - ⟩ Recommendations for Early Childhood Educators
        - · Establish Reciprocal Relationships with Families, Item 3: Be curious, making time to learn about the families with whom you work.
    - ⟩ Recommendations for Administrators of Schools, Centers, Family Child Care Homes, and Other Early Childhood Education Settings
        - · Item 9: Create meaningful, ongoing opportunities for multiple voices with diverse perspectives to engage in leadership and decision making.
- "Developmentally Appropriate Practice" position statement (NAEYC 2020)
    - ⟩ Guideline 2: Engaging in Reciprocal Partnerships with Families and Fostering Community Connections, Item D: Educators acknowledge a family's choices and goals for their child and respond with sensitivity and respect to those preferences and concerns.
    - ⟩ Recommendations for Implementing Developmentally Appropriate Practice
        - · Recommendations for Schools, Family Child Care Homes, and Other Program Settings, Item H: Actively engage family members and the broader community in all aspects of program planning and implementation, recognizing and taking into account the systemic inequities that can make it difficult for members of traditionally marginalized groups to participate.

When school leaders set expectations for reciprocal family partnerships, these partnerships are cultivated on the premise of safety, trust, respect, and inclusion. As families begin to trust that educators care about and believe in their children, they will be more willing to open up about their hopes, beliefs, and concerns (Derman-Sparks & Edwards with Goins 2020). Families that feel accepted and respected are also far more open to engaging educators in a dialogue about the program or classroom (Trivette & Keilty 2017). The respect educators show families creates the opportunity for true conversation and discussion—and for support. Instead of generalizing families to meet set "expectations" of the standard family partnership, seek to understand that each family is unique (Trivette & Keilty 2017). By doing so, children feel seen, valued, and as if their individual identities, cultures, languages, and families belong within the early learning program. "Making intentional efforts to create partnerships with families who are most at-risk, raising their voices, and expanding their opportunities to be engaged in their student learning, is a way to ensure that each and every child has the opportunity to thrive" (NAFSCE 2022, 4).

The Preschool-to-Prison Pipeline

Implicit biases are barriers to reciprocal family partnerships that often result in differential judgments of children's families and children's play and abilities. For example, "these biases are associated with lower rates of achievement and assignment to 'gifted' services and disproportionately higher rates of suspension and expulsion, beginning in preschool, for African American children, especially boys" (NAEYC 2019, 15). Another consequence of implicit biases includes the preschool-to-prison pipeline, a process that pushes children out of school through strict disciplinary measures, such as suspensions and expulsions, and into a path with a higher likelihood of involvement with the criminal justice system. This process disproportionately affects children of color. The preschool-to-prison pipeline runs from preschool through elementary school settings and beyond in which children of color mentally drop out of school because of educators' and the early learning program's implicit biases, low expectations of the child and the child's family, and lack of initiative to partner with the child's family; expulsion; and educational boredom and failure (Camera 2021; Rashid 2009).

A critical factor to countering the preschool-to-prison pipeline is evaluating a school's policies and practices related to the microsystem and mesosystem of Bronfenbrenner's ecological theory. As Henderson and colleagues (2007) stated, "when families are engaged in positive ways, rather than labeled as problems, schools can be transformed from places where only certain students prosper to ones where all children do well" (254). Thus, one of the most important solutions to countering the preschool-to-prison pipeline is to build trust, collaborate, and partner with diverse families.

Families know their children best. They bring knowledge about their children's cultures, languages, values, behaviors, expectations, experiences, interests, talents, likes, and dislikes. The knowledge they bring extends beyond the surface level culture—what is visible and observable, such as food, dress, music, and holidays—and instead, once trusting relationships are built, can include deep level culture—what is not visible or observable, such as values, communication styles, attitudes (Hammond 2015). Understanding how these factors impact families' engagement with the early learning program and children's development and learning is critical to taking responsibility to reflect and act on inequitable structural systems to counter the preschool-to-prison pipeline. Catalyzing change among inequitable institutional practices starts with educators recognizing they need the support from each of the families they serve and taking the necessary steps to evaluate their family partnership expectations and routines. Programs that do so embrace the belief that "all families can—and do—support their children's success" (Henderson et al. 2007, 242) and that creating reciprocal family partnerships with all families is possible. In return, unexcused absences, boredom, disengagement, suspensions, and expulsions decrease, while a sense of belonging, appreciation, and safety is promoted for all children and their families.

Successful family partnerships that have countered the preschool-to-prison pipeline provide high expectations for children, intentionally build relationships with children and their families, individualize expectations, and share power to promote empowerment of the early learning program community (Conchas 2006; Fashola 2005; Henderson et al. 2007; Nieto 2004). These early learning programs provide a welcoming and inclusive climate that is conducive to learning and provide a sense of purpose and acceptance (Lipsitz & West 2006).

A Strengths-Based Approach

As discussed, anti-bias education challenges educators to reflect on their biases and beliefs that do not respect and support families (Hill, Newton, & Williams 2017). It also encourages educators to learn more about each families' strengths, talents, and surface (e.g., foods, holidays) and deep (e.g., roles of children, ideas about education) cultures to build genuine partnerships (Derman-Sparks & Edwards with Goins 2020). Families are observant and recognize when their talents, skills, and decisions aren't respected or included and when outcomes are not fair and equitable.

A *strengths-based approach* emphasizes "people's ability to be their own agents of change and is applied by creating conditions for people to identify, value, and mobilize their strengths, capacities, and resources" (Fenton et al. 2014, 31). In this approach, the focus is on what a family can do (strengths) versus what a family cannot or is not doing (deficits).

FAMILY VOICES

Developmental Needs and Remote Solutions

For my daughter, remote learning was a challenge. She really needed to be with that support of other students and to have that teacher right there. Even though I'm a teacher—I teach first grade—I wasn't her third grade teacher, and I myself had to learn a lot too. I think that during that time, we got to see how my daughter struggled with focus and attention. Now that the kids are back in school in our area, in the classroom building, teachers are able to see and parents are more aware of what kind of students their children are. Her fourth grade teacher noticed that there could possibly be a focus struggle for my daughter. We are currently doing the steps to get her evaluated for possible [attention-deficit/hyperactivity disorder]. Her struggle is math, and the teacher knows it's hard for her to process the lessons in class. We're very thankful that we have a teacher, a classroom environment, who's very much aware of including and making a comfortable environment for the students. She herself, as a parent, has a child who has special needs, and so she, as a parent, knows how it feels to advocate for her own child and be in those IEP and special ed meetings. She's very aware of the needs of kids who are different learners.

I think to effectively partner as a teacher with a parent and as a parent with a teacher is you have to have some kind of understanding of our roles. Being that her teacher is also a parent and also a parent of a child who has special needs, she can empathize a lot. She knows that it's not easy and there's no quick way, that we're all trying to do what's best. I also believe that a good teacher, they really need to focus on what is working with the student, praise them, think about ways to modify the work, to break it down so that that particular learner—my daughter and other students who need the lessons to be given in a different way—that they're thinking of ways to reach out to those students.

—Asian mother in a family with two children, one of whom has special learning needs

Furthermore, in an anti-bias education, strengths-based approach, educators are committed to examining the decisions they make, the words they choose, the tone they use, and the body language they present because they understand that the messages sent to families through these channels—and many others—determine whether they trust educators enough to partner with them. "Part of valuing all children and their families is to use strengths-based inclusive language in all communications that affirms individuality and reflects an understanding of context" (NAEYC 2022, 58). For example, imagine there is a child in your class who repeatedly arrives to school late, in his pajamas, and not fed. What are your initial thoughts about the family? Many might automatically think that the child's family is incapable of preparing their child for the learning environment or being on time. When relying on a strengths-based approach, however, an educator would step back from any assumptions and seek to understand the challenges this family might be facing in getting their child to the program in the morning. The strengths-based approach focuses on and builds on the strengths, talents, skills, and interests a family brings to the table (Erdman & Colker with Winter 2020) versus the deficits, or what a family is perceived as lacking or not contributing to the classroom or program. As Bryan and Henry (2008) explain, a strengths-based approach

> treats the students and their parents with respect and care, recognizes families as valuable assets and powerful allies in their children's education, and believes that the school exists to serve families and the community. In addition, they work hard to foster a nurturing and positive environment for students and a warm, welcoming climate for all parents. (150)

A deficit mindset views specific families as broken, uneducated, limited by their abilities and resources, and dysfunctional, and therefore in need of fixing and education. An example of a deficit mindset is providing a workshop to families on a topic such as "how to talk to your child at home" without involving families in a discussion about their needs and wants regarding workshop topics or in planning the format of the workshop. A strengths-based approach, on the other hand, recognizes and celebrates the varied ways families speak to their children (e.g., singing, storytelling) and invites families to share these methods. "It is imperative that we listen to each and every family, observe their practices, and approach a partnership from an asset perspective" (Knight 2022, 69). In this approach, there is an understanding that families are doing the best they can within their unique circumstances. Educators do not judge families on what they are "not doing correctly." A strengths-based approach is an "ecological perspective that stresses the importance of examining people's characteristics, the type of environment they live in, and the multiple contexts that influence their lives [. . .] particularly by empowering clients rather than labeling them" (Saint-Jacques, Turcotte, & Pouliot 2009, 454). The assets families bring to the learning environment are appreciated and integrated into the school and classroom. This model recognizes that families have the skill and knowledge to support their children's development and learning (Trivette & Keilty 2017) and leverages each family's strengths. This model values the importance of intentionally "seeking information from families and communities about their social and cultural beliefs and practices to supplement your knowledge" (NAEYC 2019, 6). In other words, families are priceless assets and experts in meeting the needs of their child.

Moreover, using anti-bias education and a strengths-based approach as frameworks, along with knowledge about child development, helps to support and inform an educator's philosophy on reciprocal family partnerships, recognizing that all families have strengths and funds of knowledge. Educators must create opportunities where each family feels safe; a sense of belonging; and that they are respected, expected, and empowered to partner and collaborate with their child's early learning program and teacher. Thus, it is educators' job to eradicate the experiences many families have encountered in learning environments that have unintentionally set up barriers to developing reciprocal collaboration and partnerships. These barriers impact families' perception of school and classroom inclusion and partnership. Dismantling such barriers requires an ongoing commitment—"both individually and collectively—to continuous learning based on personally reflecting on how our beliefs, biased, and actions have been shaped by our experiences of the systems of privilege and oppression in which we operate and based on respectfully listening to others' perspectives" (NAEYC 2019, 4).

Incorporating a strengths-based approach takes "advantage of the additive effects of blending professional knowledge and skills with the strengths of the family through reciprocal partnership" (Trivette & Keilty 2017, vi). A strengths-based approach to reciprocal family partnerships embraces and includes each family's funds of knowledge.

Table 2.3. What Communication in Reciprocal Family Partnerships Looks Like

With families of infants and toddlers	Dialogue with families about their preferred method(s) of communication to receive updates, notices, pictures, and videos (e.g., email, texts, face-to-face conversations). Create a family communication logbook to record these responses and ensure that the desired form of communication is used.
With families of preschoolers	Support families in their children's development and learning through ongoing collaboration. The prekindergarten years are foundational and transitional years. Remain accessible to families when their children are ages 3 and 4 years. "To build on that common ground, look for ways to create dialogue with each family, where you listen and learn as well as talk" (Derman-Sparks & Edwards with Goins 2020, 67). Ensure you look for ways to create ongoing dialogue at least weekly. Keep a family communication record of the date/time, dialogue, and next steps/action steps.
With families of kindergartners	Ask families to create a video or send you a home video that describes or demonstrates their child's personality and characteristics, including their early education experiences, interests, hobbies, and strengths. Allow families to use video recordings as a form of communication throughout the year. Remain flexible in communicating and responding using their preferred method of communication, such as recorded video messages.
With families of children in the first through third grades	Engage families in dialogue about their hopes and dreams for their child. Listen to them to understand their goals and their needs.

An anti-bias education, strengths-based approach to reciprocal family partnerships requires ongoing reflection and action:

> **Reflection.** Reflective practice is required to achieve equitable opportunities for families and their children. As research related to child development and family engagement continues to change and evolve, educators must be willing to seek professional knowledge that will address the realities of the families they serve. Furthermore, educators must be open to personal growth and a willingness to change their beliefs and assumptions as they continue to acquire knowledge. Reflect on the importance of developing trust, developing a team or partnership, the role of the teacher and the practices they use, and the time and process it takes to co-create an effective reciprocal family partnership.

> **Action.** *Advocacy* is defined as the process of supporting a person, group, or cause (Grant & Ray 2016). Advocating for diverse families and their children takes courage. It requires self-reflection, acknowledgement of biases, attention to exhibited behaviors, and a willingness to be vulnerable and uncomfortable. You must be committed and open to critically examine the inequities that stem from historical, social, cultural, and linguistic misconceptions. Advocacy elicits an action response that propels change. Activism requires a collective body of like-minded stakeholders to take action and lead efforts with the goal of creating change around a specific issue (Williams 2019). An activist advocates for change through their actions. Early childhood educators take action through the early learning program and classroom environment they create, the curriculum they develop, and the instructional and assessment practices they use.

FAMILY VOICES

Equitable Expectations

Bweikia Steen: What are the characteristics you look for in your child's (or children's) teachers?

Minerva (Black mother in a two-parent family with two children): We are looking for a teacher that is fair and equitable, [one] that provides our kids with the same care and attention that she gives all of the kids. One of the things I have an eye out for at the beginning of the year is whether or not this teacher has bought into the stereotype that African American boys are not as smart and that they will never achieve as high as their White counterparts. They have low expectations for African American boys. I'm looking for that.

Bweikia Steen: What are you looking for when you say you're looking for that?

Minerva: I'm looking to see if my son provides mediocre work back to her. She says, "Oh, that's okay," when it's not okay. I'm looking to see if there's a type of special treatment for the White kids. Just call it what it is.

Every child under an early childhood educator's care deserves opportunities to achieve their fullest potential possible; this means that educators must intentionally and consistently evaluate their biases and behaviors to ensure that each family feels respected, valued, safe, and heard. Families are aware and observant and can name the injustices and inequalities that occur within their child's learning environment. Maslow's hierarchy of needs states that humans have basic needs, and these needs motivate actions (McLeod 2020). Developing trusting and supportive partnerships with diverse families starts by understanding that programs must meet the basic needs of families, including physiological, security, social, and esteem needs. These needs range from food and shelter, to feeling included and involved by using their strengths and talents, to feeling appreciated, respected, and validated for the contributions they bring to the program and classroom. Satisfying the basic needs is important in order to avoid unpleasant feelings. Dismantling and reconstructing policies, practices, and beliefs that have marginalized diverse families is a big task but not unattainable. An anti-bias education and strengths-based approach to education explicitly works to end all forms of bias and discrimination (NAEYC 2019).

Commit to Listening, Learning, and Reflecting

Taking into account the family engagement core competencies outlined by NAFSCE (reflect, connect, collaborate, and lead) and the themes that have emerged from the many dialogues I have had with diverse families, I have identified three criteria that educators must commit to when developing reciprocal family partnerships: (1) listen to families, (2) learn from and with families, and (3) reflect on the knowledge acquired from families to evaluate bias and preconceived perceptions of families. Each of these criteria places the child and the family at the center of all decisions related to policies and practices.

Listen to families. It is important that families know their voices are valued, are invited to share their voices, and have acquired the trust through an inclusive and safe school culture to use their voices. "Dialogue engages people in building their understanding of an issue, without the pressure to make decisions or be 'right'" (Graybill & Easton 2015, n.p.). When initiating dialogue with families, remember to accept families where they are. This means you might have to make multiple attempts to communicate, build trust, and establish relationships with families. This is particularly true for families who may have experienced school-based trauma and may no longer trust the school setting. Don't give up. Continue to work on building the trust necessary to develop a relationship that forms into a reciprocal family partnership.

> Some families are at ease talking with teachers and are comfortable raising issues of concern about the educational program. Some families, at least initially, wouldn't consider raising issues of concern, much less challenging a school policy or a teacher's practice, because they believe that a teacher is to be respected and obeyed. Most families experience teachers as being in a position to judge their child and their parenting, rather than as partners in fostering their children's development and learning. (Derman-Sparks & Edwards with Goins 2020, 67)

Trust is defined as confidence that another person will act in a way to benefit or sustain the relationship, or the implicit or explicit goals of the relationship, to achieve positive outcomes for children through reciprocal communication, collaboration, positive climate, organizational citizenship, collective efficacy, and equitable achievement (Tschannen-Moran & Hoy 2000). The process of developing a trusting relationship that forms into a supportive and reciprocal partnership requires full staff involvement. Trust the process. Over time, you will see the value and results of your family partnership efforts (Koralek, Nemeth, & Ramsey 2019).

Learn from and with families. Acquire developmental, cultural, linguistic, and racial competence with "wonder and curiosity" (Knight 2022, 73). Be open to learning about and from families, receiving constructive feedback, and reflecting on the similarities and differences between your norms and funds of knowledge and those of the families and communities you serve. In addition, examine the role unconscious bias plays in equitable access and opportunity. Take time to listen to and learn from families to evaluate what is and isn't working to determine ways to collaborate and advocate for young children and their families. This intentional desire to learn about each family's culture, experiences, skills, successes, and challenges helps to cultivate an understanding about how best to support the development of the child. Educators should consider the following action steps:

> Analyze the mission, vision, and policies related to partnerships with the families and the communities served. Do families know the early learning program's vision and mission? Is it time to revisit the vision and mission? Is the program's vision and mission inclusive of all families' voices? Is it inclusive and equitable for all young children and their families?

> Include, embrace, and acknowledge diverse families. Identify the families who are and are not involved, participating, and engaged with the early learning program. Intentionally recognize, reach out, and seek to understand from those families who are not. Outreach should include a team of intentional members (e.g., school leaders, staff, teachers, other families) asking families about their preferred method of communication. Determine which communication, involvement, participation, and engagement strategies are necessary to support and connect with each family.

> Request families' ideas and opinions through ongoing dialogues, surveys, and questionnaires. Collate and review that information, and implement changes based on it. The more the families see that their voices matter and elicit change, the sooner they will trust the process and be willing to partner with the early learning program team.

Reflect on the knowledge acquired from families to evaluate bias and preconceived perceptions of families. Effective early learning programs understand that reciprocal family partnerships are built on skilled dialogues that respect a range of diverse perspectives, make space for equitable interactions that allow voices for all perspectives, and lead to a response that accesses and taps into the strengths of diverse perspectives (Barrera & Corso 2002). They dedicate time and take the steps to evaluate all staff members' biases and perceptions related to family partnerships. "Early educators must be mindful of how our experiences and cultural backgrounds have shaped us" (Knight 2022, 73). It is critical to recognize that negative perceptions and attitudes can lead to detrimental outcomes for diverse children. NAEYC's (2020) position statement on developmentally appropriate practice suggests that teachers and school leaders enter into classrooms and early learning programs with expectations about reciprocal family partnerships. These expectations are based on personal experiences, including those based on dominant social and cultural norms and expectations and first-hand, personal interactions with specific families.

"Well, I don't know. We might have to kick him out of school."

I interviewed the mother of a 5-year-old boy who had started at an early learning program for the first time. He had never been in a classroom setting, and he was an only child. The mother's experiences with the teacher and program caused her stress and anxiety. I asked her, "Is there anything that is not working with your family regarding your child's school or with your child's teacher, and what would you propose as the solution to remedy the situation?" This is that mother's story.

I am a mom to a 5-year-old little boy who is in kindergarten. I originally wanted to homeschool him, but after weighing the pros and cons, and just being a single mom, I decided that it would be best for us at the moment if I put him in public school. About a week before school started, I met with his teacher. I wanted to get to know her, and for her to know me. He started school on a Tuesday, and on Friday I started getting calls from his teacher talking about his behavior in class.

Mind you, my son had never been in a structured environment at all. [The teacher] asked a lot of questions, but it was never, "What was his prior experience with being around other kids?" Though he had some, it was an ongoing thing. He wasn't in daycare—he wasn't in anything like that—and so I kept him home with me. He is an only child. She suggested that maybe he had mental or emotional health issues. She said she was trying to just figure out if he was just spoiled or what was going on. She even said—this was the first four days of school—she was like, "Well, I don't know. We might have to kick him out of school."

I was stressed. The phone calls kept coming. I went up to the school to talk to the [principal and vice principal]. It was like he was the worst kid they had ever seen, or she had ever seen. Let me say that. I was just raising my concerns and trying to figure out, "What do you do, and what happens when you have kids like this that are having a hard time adjusting to a new environment and to structure, and having many kids around them, and all that kind of stuff? What happens? How do you deal with this?"

I found out later, [the teacher] would kick him out of the classroom. That meant he was missing that structure, that learning time. He wasn't in the classroom learning. That became a very big concern as well. It was like, "What can you do in the classroom to keep him there so that he is not missing this time of learning?" I would ask him every day—I was concerned about him being labeled. I was concerned about him being seen as the problem child or the problem student.

Instead of maybe adjusting or really trying to learn and figure out how [they] can reach him, it was again that, "We'll take him out of the classroom, and I won't have to deal with you." When my son would come home, I would ask him, "How did your day go? What was everything about, or how was everything?" He would tell me, "My teacher tells me she doesn't love me when I act this way." That was concerning because I think for her, she was trying to say something to him and try to manipulate him into the behavior that she wanted him to do.

—Black mother who is a single parent with a 5-year-old child

This mom offers some concrete strategies and ideas for how the teachers and early learning program could engage with families and work together as a team. It's important to listen to families not only to learn about their children, but also to learn about who they are, how they communicate, what their routines and schedules are, and what their concerns and needs are. School leaders and teachers cannot make decisions about family engagement in a vacuum. They need to partner and work with the families as a team to develop strategies that are reflective, effective, and meaningful.

Truly advocating for young children and their families requires that you ask yourself the following questions:

1. How am I supporting each family's unique cultural background?

2. Am I striving to learn about my families' diverse parenting practices?

3. Do I consider cultural practices when assessing children's growth and development?

4. Am I aware of my own explicit and implicit biases, and do I take time to reflect on these? (Knight 2022, 74)

Summary

To disrupt the exclusionary practices many diverse families face, early childhood educators must be willing to reflect on norms, biases, and assumptions; evaluate the research about child development and the importance of understanding each child's funds of knowledge; and engage in dialogues with families to develop trusting relationships that lead to advocating for all families and that evolve to form reciprocal family partnerships. Understanding the many influences on children and how each layer intersects and relates to impact their development can help educators and family members overcome barriers to successful partnerships (Yamauchi et al. 2017). This requires a commitment to seeking appropriate knowledge about families' cultures and their funds of knowledge. Furthermore, early learning programs must recognize the negative effects that focusing on deficits rather than strengths has on their work with families. All families need equitable opportunities to receive acknowledgement, support, and respect (NAEYC 2019). A child's education begins with their family, so connecting with the family will give insight into meeting that child's overall needs. Consciously involving, engaging, and incorporating families into the early learning program and classroom community helps to inform instructional decisions and practices.

Relationships and partnerships with families depend on your ability to develop the stance of continuously working to engage, involve, and include all families, no matter what. It is a commitment to saying, "I will work to reflect on my actions and biases and to create equitable opportunities for all families." Furthermore, it depends on your ability to set aside assumptions and to be open to learning about each family as the unique group of individuals they are (Koralek, Nemeth, & Ramsey 2019). Reciprocal family partnerships are built on the principles of developmentally appropriate practice as well as anti-bias education and a strengths-based approach. They take time, teamwork, and patience, but they are transformative and positively impact outcomes for all key stakeholders involved.

Reflect

1. What did you read in this chapter that surprised you? That affirmed your ideas and practices? That made you want to learn more?

This chapter supports the following:

 NAEYC Early Learning Program Accreditation Standards and Topic Areas

Standard 1: Relationships

1.A Building Positive Relationships Between Educators and Families

1.B Building Positive Relationships Between Educators and Children

 Professional Standards and Competencies for Early Childhood Educators

Standard 2: Family-Teacher Partnerships and Community Connections

2a: Know about, understand, and value the diversity of families.

2b: Collaborate as partners with families in young children's development and learning through respectful, reciprocal relationships and engagement.

Hear Our Voices! Engaging in Partnerships that Honor Families

CHAPTER 3

Creating a Caring Community and Welcoming Environment

Guiding Questions

As you read this chapter, consider the following:

1. Think about a time when you felt welcomed and included in an event, committee, or organization. What things made you feel this way?

2. In your opinion, what is the role of the school and classroom environments in including and supporting families? How do these environments contribute to the creation of reciprocal family partnerships?

3. What role does trust play in building relationships with families and cultivating an inclusive school culture and climate?

FAMILY VOICES

With my son—again, pre-pandemic—at 9 months old he started at this really lovely space. The provider put so much thought into every decision of the space. Even entering, all parents had to remove their shoes. There were books lined up on parenting and schooling and different educational philosophies. The environment was so important. She was incredibly conscientious about the forming of a safe, nurturing space for parents, as well as children.

—Latina mother, part of a two-parent family with two toddler-age children

---

From the moment a family member enters the school building or program center, they should feel welcome as part of the learning community. In a learning environment that embraces an anti-bias education and strengths-based approach, families have ongoing and varied opportunities to collaborate with educators. The culture of a child's classroom and of the wider learning community cultivates trusting relationships with families by demonstrating that belonging, safety, and respect are core principles that guide practices and methods for inclusion. This type of environment also recognizes that all families have identities, cultures, experiences, and circumstances that influence how they view and interact with educators.

For example, my mother was a single Black mother of two daughters. She worked three jobs to support my sister and me. Although she understood the importance of volunteering in the classroom and advocating for her children, her circumstances prevented her from attending educational events and engaging with the early learning program in the ways deemed traditional and appropriate by the school system. These barriers did not afford her the privilege to regularly access our learning environment. Part of creating a caring community and welcoming environment means seeking to understand and consider each family's circumstances in order to eliminate barriers that stand in the way of partnerships and determine equitable and appropriate ways to ensure all families are heard and seen. This chapter discusses the *why* and the *how* of creating positive cultures and climates that honor all families.

School Culture and Climate

All organizations have a culture that is defined by its underlying values and beliefs. The organization's actions, communications, and interactions with key stakeholders, including clients, staff, and the larger community, express this culture. Early learning programs likewise have cultures that can determine the extent to which families engage with their child's education. Bloom and Abel (2015) explain it as follows:

> The culture of an early childhood setting is what makes it unique. Culture includes the shared values, assumptions, and collective beliefs about what is important, and the norms and expectations for what is appropriate and acceptable in everyday interactions. Culture also includes the traditions, rituals, celebrations, and customs that distinguish one program or school from another. An early childhood setting's organizational climate is slightly different from its culture. Organizational climate is the staff's collective perceptions of what the organization is like in terms of policies, practices, procedures, and routines. Culture and climate are complementary concepts with overlapping, yet distinguishable, nuances of organizational life. (11)

A school's culture also includes the policies it adopts and relates to the mission and vision. In a nutshell, culture is *how* things are done, whereas climate is how stakeholders *feel* about the way things are. "Culture goes deeper to include the immediate environment and what people believe and value" (Joseph 2022, n.p.). When the culture and climate are built on mutual respect and partnership, the entire learning community benefits. This harkens back to trust between leadership and other staff, particularly school leaders and teachers in the classroom.

While culture and climate are different, making both positive and inclusive requires an ongoing process of intentionality based on shared beliefs from all stakeholders. The culture and climate signal to families who belongs and who doesn't throughout all aspects of the school—in classrooms, in hallways, at the front office, in the curriculum, in assessments, in goals and their prioritization, and more. These messages impact the environment and create conditions that inform the extent of involvement, engagement, and partnership among families.

From the Perspective of a Teacher and a Parent

As far as getting families involved, I do feel like we could be reaching out more as a school district as well, like getting parents more into interventions. Like educational nights for the parents where we share, "This is the kind of strategy you could be working on with your child. Here are some tools. Here are some take-homes. Here are some things that you could be doing." I know a few times over my teaching career we have done that, and I find that they're very powerful for the parents. I don't think that there was enough of that outreach and intervention. With the caseload that we have, it's really hard for us to make that happen individually as teachers, but if it was built into the system, like on back-to-school nights or a monthly teacher-parent education night, that would probably help parents feel more comfortable coming to us with questions. It would help us feel like we're being more effective.

—White mother, early childhood educator and part of a single-parent family with one child who has a disability

It Starts with Leadership

School leaders set the tone and model expectations for the entire learning community. The learning community looks to and takes cues from the words and actions of the school leader. Everything from the way leaders greet each family, to their interactions with teachers and staff, to how they manage day-to-day business (such as prioritizing funding, providing appropriate resources, and meeting state and district mandates), is critical to the school's culture and climate.

This community consists of everyone who enters the school setting. It can include, but is not limited to, the following:

> Families

> Teachers (e.g., full-time teachers, instructional assistants, substitute teachers, tutors)

> School leaders (e.g., program directors, principals, administrators)

> General school staff (e.g., activities coordinators, cafeteria workers, custodians, librarians, office administrators, school nurses)

> Specialists (e.g., counselors and psychologists, early interventionists, health professionals, special education professionals)

> Community members, organizations, and programs (e.g., case and social workers, high schoolers, language interpreters, libraries, neighbors, parks and recreation services, local clubs)

The school community functions best as a team. Therefore, each person should know and feel that they are part of the community and be seen as a key stakeholder in the success of the program and its children. Everyone has the same goal: helping children to grow and thrive. School leaders, teachers, and staff members create opportunities for other stakeholders to feel welcomed and heard when taking part in these processes. "Children learn and develop best when all participants in a community consider and contribute to one another's well-being and learning and are valued for the strengths they bring" (NAEYC 2022, 111).

School leaders must build the capacity of teachers and staff to meet the expectations and standards required to contribute to a positive, welcoming, and equitable culture and climate (NAEYC 2019). Provide time, space, and ongoing opportunities throughout the year to learn about, reflect on, discuss, and create action steps related to this work and how it develops reciprocal family partnerships. Time and incentives should also be given to encourage teachers and staff to participate in opportunities such as book clubs or community connection projects where they can collaborate and reflect on learning more about families (Soule 2020).

The school community must come together to evaluate current family policies and practices, identifying those that ostracize nondominant families, or those families "impacted by systemic oppression, such as marginalization based on race, class, language, or immigration status" (Ishimaru 2020, 8). They must also establish policies and practices that are inclusive and that build on the strengths of all families served.

Connecting families. School leaders and teachers play a critical role in connecting families to the program, their child's classroom, resources, and other families within the learning community. Connecting families to each other in particular cultivates a sense of belonging, camaraderie, and safety, which leads to trust. It helps to provide another dimension of support, empowerment, and advocacy through intentional community building. That said, educators must recognize that there are multiple ways to connect families to one another—look beyond just language and race similarities. For example, you might connect families who have children who are in the same grade level or classroom; who have the same advocacy needs; or who share the same interests, hobbies, or occupations. Create these connections through intentional introductions (e.g., offering times during school activities for families to mingle and connect with one another) or informally during drop-off and pickup.

FAMILY VOICES

Be Present and Engaged

We do have a new school principal. She came from a school that was literally around the corner, another elementary school, and from my understanding, she was excellent. From what I have seen from meeting her, she is very much engaged. She's always there in the mornings outside greeting the kids and families and helping the other teachers.

—Mother of a family with four children

The House System for Building Family and School Teamwork

Traditionally, a *house system* is a practice in which the school divides children into groups (or "houses") that compete and are rewarded for good behavior and accomplishments (Staake 2018). It is most common in the United Kingdom, especially in boarding schools, though it has spread to the United States. I have observed a learning community adapt the house system as a vehicle for furthering reciprocal family partnerships. Each grade level created several houses and invited families to collaborate with teams of teachers to develop community among the houses instead of fostering competition. Three times per year, each house came together for a school-wide community-building party.

Working with the larger community. "Establish collaborative relationships with other social service agencies and providers within the community" (NAEYC 2019, 9). All stakeholders in the early learning program have a continuum of needs that influence their well-being, including academic or professional development, social and emotional, and physical. Meeting these needs means connecting with leaders and organizations within the community who can provide resources, opportunities, and other supports. Dialogue with families, staff, and the school community to identify appropriate and sustainable partnerships within the wider community. For example, a school leader of an early childhood elementary school partnered with the local Walmart to secure clothing for children to wear after a spill or other accident. The leader stated that this partnership was important because she knew that many of the children's families commuted to jobs that were several hours away; asking them to return to the school to provide clothing for their children was unrealistic. Engaging the larger community also offers opportunities to conduct program-related activities in locations outside of the school building.

As with any team in which the individuals rely on other members for work and support, all relationships in the learning community are connected—they influence and are influenced by each other. For example, the kind of relationship that exists between a school leader and a teacher and the qualities that characterize that relationship (e.g., level of trust, attention to teacher well-being, degree of communication, level of teacher autonomy) can impact the relationship that a teacher, in turn, has with a child and their family.

"Without system-wide leadership support, strong family engagement practices and innovations will gain little traction and will evaporate with shifts in interest and personnel" (Mapp & Bergman 2021, 15). Effective school leaders understand this, but they also understand that they cannot single-handedly carry out the work necessary to create a culture and climate that is built on relationships, connections, and collaboration. Working in a silo leads to missed opportunities for rich engagement and interactions that capitalize on each stakeholder's expertise (Mellott 2021). A leader who embraces developmentally appropriate practice, anti-bias education, and a strengths-based approach intentionally collaborates with the whole learning community to ensure the inclusion and celebration of diverse perspectives within decision making and goal setting. This means the school leader prioritizes time to identify policies and practices that are not inclusive, provides opportunities for stakeholders to reflect on and discuss these policies and practices, and addresses any inequities that are perpetuated.

Tips for Making All Families Feel Welcome and Included

1. **Greet families at the front door during drop-off, pickup, and events.** Consider each encounter with families as a chance to make a great impression and build on your connection. Smile, say "Hello" or "Good morning (afternoon)," and initiate informal conversations. This etiquette is important to stick to even if a family is late dropping their child off, has just cut in line at pickup, or never responds to communication. You never know what a family has gone through to get their child to school.

2. **Encourage staff to make the same quantity and quality of effort in building relationships with all families.** Just as educators intentionally do not play "favorites" with children, the same must be true for the children's families. Families are observant, and they know when the front office staff, the school leader, or their child's teacher shows preferential treatment to some families over others. Be aware of your behavior and actions toward families. All interactions must be individualized yet equitable.

3. **Encourage families to build relationships with each other.** Although your influence in this capacity might be limited, you can still create opportunities to promote collaboration and a sense of community among all families. Some families may marginalize others, intentionally or unintentionally. They might do so by selectively communicating and engaging with specific families (e.g., consistently greeting certain family members waiting alongside them in the pickup line while ignoring others, inviting only specific families to events). Be aware of the climate and families who have a tendency to be cliquish. During family events coordinated by the early learning program, use various strategies to encourage families to mix it up and interact with different families.

4. **Include and encourage men as active participants.** Men in education are rare, but their presence is important. Intentionally seek ways to engage and include men throughout the learning community. For example, the men of an elementary school in Virginia created a Dads Club. The members created t-shirts to wear when working in the school building, attended monthly meetings, and recruited other men to volunteer and serve in various capacities within the school: hallway monitor, lunch monitor, recess monitor, reader in specific classrooms, and tutor. The school leader dedicated a bulletin board in the hallway to the Dads Club. Each week, they added new pictures and videos of the men to the bulletin board.

5. **Partner with local retirement centers.** Members of the retirement community can volunteer and serve in various capacities within the school setting. Children can read to the volunteers or attend field trips to the retirement center.

The actions displayed by the school leaders, teachers, and staff demonstrate to each family that they are valued members of a caring community. Consequently, the choices leaders and teachers make and the subsequent outcomes build and strengthen relationships and promote families' trust in the learning community. The Division for Early Childhood (DEC; 2014) states that educators must engage in "practices that treat families with dignity and respect; are individualized, flexible, and responsive to each family's unique circumstances; provide family members complete and unbiased information to make informed decisions; and involve family members in acting on choices to strengthen child, parent, and family functioning" (10). This recommendation is rooted in an understanding that trusting reciprocal family partnerships are the foundation to constructing and cultivating inclusive learning environments for all families.

An environment that honors families, regardless of their identities and circumstances, seeks to counter oppressive and marginalized practices. It creates safe spaces that intentionally accept a wide understanding of what partnership looks like. In this type of environment, families are invited to unapologetically ask questions, engage, interact, and partner in ways that work for them in their own time. To create this environment, educators must first acknowledge that current policies and practices leave certain families excluded, which can lead to mistrust between the home and early learning program. This is especially true for nondominant families. Then, educators must articulate, incorporate, and enforce mission, vision, and goal statements that will reduce systemic barriers and illuminate the unique strengths of each family.

Communication

A school's culture is evident in the way its leaders, teachers, and staff communicate with families, each other, and the community. School leaders set communication standards and policies, and when leaders communicate proactively and positively with families, it sets the tone for the learning community as a whole. For example, one early childhood administrator would send a welcome email and text to families before the start of the school year that read, "Thank you for sending us your very best: your child. At our school, we work together to take care of your child." This simple gesture helps make families feel welcome and important and sets an example for teachers and staff. Classroom teachers are the key communicators with the families because, as Jung and Sheldon (2020) describe, "teachers are best positioned to have consistent interactions and maintain the closest relationships with families" (11). It is teachers who are with the children day in and day out, observing how they learn and develop. They have the information that each family wants and deserves to know. Positive, proactive, and regular communication helps to break down the barriers that hinder families' access to the school and classroom. It is important to note that "being in communication with families is not the same as being in a relationship with them" (Charania 2021, 8). Rather, it is just one strategy to build trusting relationships with families.

Because culture and previous experiences inform the level of trust families have in the school system—and inform their behavior and engagement with educators—you should reflect on and evaluate your communication expectations and methods. Establishing effective communication is an ongoing process. Your mindset and attitude must be flexible, and you must be willing to put in the effort and commitment to use multiple communication strategies.

What Is the Best Environment for Any Child?

Taraji (Black mother, part of a two-parent, blended, military family with three children): Family partnership is when, at the school, they are aware of your goals for your child as parents. They're interested in knowing what your goals are, you know what the school's goals are, and they're open about what their goals for your child's development are. You have a sense of shared goals, and you have a sense of each other's roles. As the parent, I know my contribution to those goals and the school's aware of that.

Bweikia Steen: What type of school environment is your daughter in and how did you choose it?

Taraji: She is at a small center. We knew that she would be in a space where she'd get plenty of individual attention. We really like the small setting that she would be in—and just full honesty—during a pandemic. With partnership and what it's looked like, when she was younger, it was just swapping tips. For example, just a teacher saying when she is learning her letters, it's not just singing your ABCs but putting ABCs in front of her so she sees them. As she's gotten older, those tips aren't just based on learning, but I feel like our partnership is around her social-emotional development more so now. For example, hearing from them that she does a lot of crying. It's her response to transition. If she's playing and it's time to go outside, if she's outside and it's time to come inside, she is a waterworks type of little girl. Knowing that, then we can start to say to her at home, "We want to hear you use your words."

Bweikia Steen: How did the teacher or the school ensure that it was a partnership? What were the steps for you? How did you not take that kind of feedback as negative?

Taraji: I ask about the things that I see at home. One way, though, I do think that a teacher can bring it up is saying, just like I asked them, "How is she doing at using her listening ears? How is she doing at using her words instead of crying? How is she doing at going to the potty?" I'm going to ask those questions. I appreciate the same back as a parent, instead of coming to me to say, "Have you noticed these behaviors?" or instead of framing it as a disruption. Asking questions is partnership. Her teachers have been proactive about making sure there's conversation. During drop-off and pickup, we also have conversations. I don't have to wait for that formal review time.

I have a couple of things I really would like to be a bit different. One we don't have control over is COVID. With COVID, families can't go inside during drop-off and pickup. Now we're masked up; it's leave them at the door, pick them up from the door, and you're not going inside and getting a chance to engage in the classroom. I think that that has broken down some of the way I feel a partnership really works. That is, of course, not on the center. But I've been wondering about incorporating some outside play with families. Even if you didn't do it with every family, but just like, "Hey, we're offering today that you can come pick up your child a little bit early and have some time to play with them on the playground at the school." Again, just giving us a chance to know better how our children engage with their friends at school, even that five-minute time that you would be in the classroom when you pick them up. This made a difference in how connected I felt with the center. When my daughter was under 2 and couldn't really talk to me about what was happening at school, I could see it. I could see just how the teacher engages. I could learn some things: here's the type of response that this teacher has when she behaves a certain way, here's how he's teaching her to do X, Y, or Z. It helped build the partnership, it helped with trust, and it helped with a sense of community. I feel like you get to even know the teachers as people a little better because you chit-chat about their kids. There is something missing about the community feeling when you're not able to go in.

It is also important to me that my daughter has positive reflections of culture and who she is. It has caused friction between me and the school because I am pushing for different stories. My daughter is not reflected in the story of Goldilocks, and I want more diverse stories. I am seeing that, actually, because they send photos in the app that they have. We get photos of her class every day, and so we are able to see what she's doing. That builds back some of that sense of community. I am seeing that they've implemented a story time where they encourage children to bring a book from home. We're always going to send books like *I Am Black History*, *I Am Unique!*, or just different books so that we are incorporating pride in who they are as a diverse group of children. At first, there was some friction. I was really like, "Where's the positive representation that shows her? Where do we show her positive images of herself?" That just was not existing. I still have not seen it as a part of the formal curriculum.

What Is Communicated?

Communication between families and educators "can be structural (i.e., focused on school practices or information) or relational (i.e., focused on interpersonal dynamics such as trust)" (Sheridan et al. 2020, 367). When it comes to structural communications, educators must "communicate clear, comprehensive, and objective information about resources and supports that help families to make informed decisions and advocate for access, participation, and equity in natural and inclusive environments" (DEC 2020, 5).

How and When Communication Is Delivered Matters

Communication extends beyond written form, such as newsletters, emails, text messages, and webpages. It includes what educators say aloud and is expressed in their body language, tone of voice, actions, and reactions. Messages are also communicated through the materials and visuals incorporated in the school and classroom environments. These speak volumes to families about whether they are valued members of the community. Be mindful of the ways these forms of communication, conscious and unconscious, impact families' sense of safety and belonging. Consider the following:

> Is language (both written and verbal) easy to understand and brief? Is educational jargon used? Are communications translated into the home language(s) of children's families?

> Is the method (e.g., emails, texts, an app) inclusive and accessible to all families? Are multiple methods used? If yes, is their purpose consistent and clear to families?

To provide equitable access to communication, use multiple formats to convey messages and leverage technology. Reaching out to families where they are is essential; this includes making use of newer avenues of communication, such as social media. For example, if families are not able to attend functions in person, you can post information covered during those events on Facebook, Instagram, or TikTok, as appropriate. In addition, making events virtually accessible via video conferencing platforms like Zoom provides yet another option for families. You can also record events and share them with families to view at their convenience (e.g., posting videos to the program's webpage, distributing via email). School-based apps are another option to consider.

Remember, when using a form of communication that is new to families (like school-based apps), it is imperative that families have opportunities to learn about it, including how to access and use it as well as how and why it will be used by educators throughout the year. I have found that many families are aware of the school-based app, but because they do not understand its function or purpose, they do not use it. Be careful not to blame families for information "they should know" because it is provided on the app. Families don't know what they don't know, and they can't be faulted for that. Depending on your geographical location or other factors, access to technology may serve as a barrier. Always adopt practices that meet the needs of the community you serve.

Just as important as what is included in the messaging is how often and quickly teachers communicate to and with families. A family will easily lose trust in a teacher or school leader if they rarely hear from them, or if their questions go unanswered. It's critical to respond to families within 24–48 hours, even if it is a simple note to say, "Hello, I received your email and will get back to you on Monday."

FAMILY VOICES

Sending Clear Messages About Bullying and Kindness

As far as communication goes, I want to know what's the school culture. After about a year and a half, I was like, "Where's the school stance on bullying?" I want to hear some mantras coming out of my kid's mouth about what the school is talking about, about kindness to one another, or what we do when we experience bullying. I want to see the counselor out there. I decided to start an inclusion and advocacy group, and then the school shared that they had a decree in terms of being kind and stuff. That's great, but my kids didn't know anything about that. I haven't seen it or heard it. I feel like culture needs to be weaved into curriculum and everything else. I would think as an administration, you want to share those messages clearly. Our kids need to be constantly hearing those things.

—White mother in a two-parent military family with three children, one of whom has a disability

Reach Out Often and in Multiple Ways

Bweikia Steen: There is a perception that Black families are hard to reach—that they don't come into school, are not engaged with their children's learning, and may not participate as much as other ethnicities. What are your thoughts about that?

Alliyah (Black mother, part of a single-parent family with one child): I think that is not true. It may have to do with parents' working schedules. It could have to do with the level of effort of the teachers and administrators in reaching out to those parents. There are several parents I'm sure that work double jobs. There are parents like me who are single parents. I'm fortunate to have my mom very involved in helping with drop-off and pickup. My mother also volunteers in the school. Some people don't have that luxury. I think that when people make these false statements, they are not taking into consideration the full picture. How much effort has that teacher made to reach out to the parents and keep the parents engaged? I seek out information on my own. Everybody doesn't know to do that. Some parents may need a little extra nudging or communicating to, but it doesn't mean they don't want to be engaged and active and involved in their child's life. It could be a simple issue of timing.

Bweikia Steen: What do you suggest that teachers and administrators do to engage Black families?

Alliyah: Reach out to them in ways that will get them to respond, whatever that may be. If it's email, if it's phone—catch the parents in the morning or during afternoon pickup! Find some way where you have a touchpoint to communicate with that parent. There are all kinds of opportunities that parents would be more than happy to engage in and learn more about how they can improve their child's education, their behavioral goals, whatever it may be.

Dismantling Barriers

Using a strengths-based approach, school leaders and teachers acknowledge that families want to be involved and engaged in their child's education; yet, they understand that there are common barriers that prevent many families from doing so. Some barriers are more obvious, such as when families have schedule conflicts due to work or other commitments. Others are more intangible, such as when a family feels mistrustful because they have been marginalized or ignored due to implicit biases. In either case, educators must work to dismantle these barriers and provide equal access to the learning community for all families.

According to Maslow's hierarchy of needs, basic needs must be fulfilled before higher-order needs can be addressed. This hierarchy goes, in ascending order (Maslow 1954)

> Physiological (e.g., food, shelter, sleep)

> Safety (e.g., security, health, structure)

> Belongingness and love (e.g., family, friendship, connection)

> Esteem (e.g., respect and esteem from others, self-respect, self-esteem)

> Self-actualization (e.g., purpose, personal growth, realization of potential)

I firmly believe that Maslow's hierarchy of needs has implications for early learning program policies and practices and must be considered when developing reciprocal family partnerships. The actions of educators speak louder than the statements displayed on a program's webpage, flyers, or newsletters. They must *show* families that their needs are considered, they belong within the learning community, they are appreciated, and the environment is a safe place to learn and grow together. Although Maslow's hierarchy of needs has been criticized for seemingly being based on Western ideologies (e.g., King-Hill 2015; Noltemeyer et al. 2021), it is important to understand the connection among basic needs, well-being, and reciprocal family partnerships, as well as the role the learning environment plays in ensuring the basic needs of children and families are realized, understood, and addressed.

FAMILY VOICES

Engaging with Families Who Reach Out

Bweikia Steen: What strategies do you think will work to bring in more parents? Or, like for the PTA, what do you think needs to happen? Are you the only Black parent?

Luisa (Black mother with one child): No, there are probably about four that rotate in and out. There's two of us that come consistently. There's a guy who started coming last year, and he's actually on the board this year. Then there's me. I'm not on the board, I'm just a member. Then you'll see—there's maybe two or three others that will come periodically, and that's pretty much it. Really, I don't think there's that many more Latina moms either. It would be great for a teacher to say, "These are ways that I'm going to support you, and these are ways that I would ask that you support me." Even with my son's teacher this year, I had to raise my hand and say, "Excuse me, how can we get in contact with you?" It was very much just, "This is the curriculum." I can see if a parent isn't normally inclined to go to the school and volunteer or read to their kid or do anything like that. Then they wouldn't have got anything from her back-to-school message or speech that would inspire them to even seek out how to do those things. I even said, "I'm willing to do math facts. I just need to know what to do. Just contact me and I need to know what to do." I've never been contacted on how to do that either. I said I'll do it, but I'm not going to keep calling and writing notes.

For instance, refer back to the first guiding question at the beginning of this chapter: *Think about a time when you felt welcomed and included in an event, committee, or organization. What things that made you feel this way?* Everyone has different experiences and needs. Some people may not need to feel welcomed within a setting to feel motivated to participate. For others, the feelings of trust and belonging—or having a meaningful voice and the opportunity to participate (Othering and Belonging Institute, n.d.)—are requirements and have implications for their level of engagement and partnership.

Now, think about Maslow's hierarchy of needs and the impact of families' unmet needs on their participation level in the school and classroom. Unmet needs have a direct impact on families' desire, will, and ability to trust and engage in these systems. For instance, families who struggle with job security, finances, and housing need a learning community, culture, and climate that serves as a safe, nonjudgmental space where they can approach educators and other stakeholders to support them. The circumstances families face might impact their ability to engage with the school, but educators cannot "pin the blame on families and obscure the school's responsibility for creating a welcoming climate for all families" (Mapp & Bergman 2021, 9). If a family is not participating in events like back-to-school nights and organizations like parent-teacher associations, there is likely a reason.

A strengths-based approach recognizes that families are doing the best they can within their circumstances (Trivette & Keilty 2017). Instead of limiting your expectations of families due to what you know about their situation or a perceived lack of engagement, recognize and honor the assets of families as critical partners in supporting their children's learning and development.

Accessibility

As has been the case for many families I've dialogued with over the years, accessibility also serves as a barrier to partnering with early learning programs. As previously mentioned, intentional school leaders recognize that all families have different needs and circumstances that may impede on their ability to participate in traditional school activities. Educators must strive to make opportunities for engagement more accessible by being receptive and responsive to families' feedback about their needs. There are concrete, practical steps educators can take to dismantle barriers and improve equity of opportunities and accessibility for diverse families. Consider the following:

1. **Access to the school and classroom settings.** Are families allowed to enter the program setting? Are they addressed upon entry? Are they allowed to ask questions at pickup or drop-off or share notes about their child's weekend or morning?

2. **Access for all diverse families, including families of color, families who speak a language other than English, and families of children with disabilities.** Are program policies and practices culturally responsive? If yes, in what ways? Where do you see gaps that need to be addressed to more effectively serve families?

Representation Is Important

I have to make my presence known at my younger son's school because what I'm experiencing now is they have a lot of younger teachers who don't look like my sons, and they don't look like me. They don't understand my children, and they don't understand how my children and other children who look like my children behave.

—Black father of a blended two-parent family with three children

The first and most important step to making the environment more accessible to families is to *ask* them. "Maintain consistently high expectations for family involvement, being open to multiple and varied forms of engagement and providing intentional and responsive supports. Ask families how they would like to be involved and what supports may be helpful" (NAEYC 2019, 8). Take every opportunity to dialogue with families to learn more about them, their well-being, their children, and the engagement practices that are or aren't working for them. In turn, invite them to share their expertise with the learning community. Ongoing and informal dialogue signals to families that their funds of knowledge are valued, respected, and appreciated. Speak with families of children with disabilities or special health care needs to understand their circumstances, which may be unique or the same as other families with young children (NAEYC 2022). (See more in "The Role of Physical Spaces" section later in this chapter.)

Make it a priority to initiate conversations with families (e.g., chat with them during drop-off or pickup, stop them in the hallways), inquire about their children, and learn the names of other family members. Often, families are limited to engaging with school leaders and teachers at predetermined times or locations, which can leave those families who can't make rigid schedules work feeling isolated. Opening up more informal and flexible options for families to connect with educators fosters trust and community (Charania 2021).

These conversations are also a source of data that is often overlooked and not seen as valuable. However, informal data about the families collected in this way is important to analyze and reflect on as a school team. Data collected through dialoguing with families provides school leaders with pertinent information related to the culture and climate and informs the changes that might need to be made. Furthermore, leaders model to the staff and each family that their voices are valued and heard.

Serving the Community You Are Part of

Minerva (Black mother in a two-parent family with two children): The classrooms last year for second grade were not balanced. They put a number of the White kids in one particular class, and then a lot of the Black boys in another classroom that happened to be the special education and ELL [English language learners] classroom. Last year was a horrible year for us.

Yuusuf (Black father in a two-parent family with two children): The teacher was brand new. That compounded the issue. They really stacked the odds against her. You had some of the students who were a bit more accelerated, who weren't challenged. A lot of the teacher's time and resources were being dedicated toward the kids who were a bit more challenged. During some of my visits to the classroom—and my wife's, she was there a lot more than me—what I saw was unbelievable. There were kids jumping across tables, running in the hallways. They were coming in and out of the classroom as they felt necessary. The teacher was unable to control the class because she wasn't provided the resources and the assistance that she needed. When there was assistance, they did try to help the situation by dedicating a lot of attention to the kids who were leaving the class—a lot of the efforts were dedicated toward behavior problems. Teaching was being undermined by the efforts to control the behavior issues.

One of the main characteristics that I look for is just a teacher that's unbiased. Sometimes, I'm guessing they just aren't aware of some of their teaching styles. Maybe they're not aware that they have approaches that aren't good for kids that come from different cultural backgrounds. For me, what I see are teachers who aren't accustomed to being around kids that come from different avenues than what they came from. It's similar to—I guess you could look at it from a law enforcement standpoint, where you've got a bunch of cops in certain neighborhoods who have no connection to the neighborhood. Teachers are the same way. You've got teachers who come from certain parts of society, and then they end up in schools that have no resemblance of where they came from. It shows when they're in the classroom in front of the kids, and the kids can tell too.

Minerva: It also shows in their communication to the parents. We would get emails from the teacher the times that our son did act up, like, "Can you please teach your son how to listen in class?" I was like, "Wait a minute." Just the whole approach was . . . just tell me what the problem is, and I know what to do. I piggyback that on what my expectation is from the administration because I think the administration needs to train the teachers on diversity, and how to communicate with different types of families. I don't know if they're getting that.

The Role of Physical Spaces

The physical environment is often the first impression families have of a learning setting. Educators should consider how the environment might appear to a family visiting for the first time. Families gain a sense of the program beginning with the outside landscaping and building maintenance. Is the grass cut and the garden cared for? Are there benches for families to sit on? Does the building appear safe and well-maintained?

Inside the building, every physical space, including hallways, classrooms, and offices, provides opportunities to create a welcoming environment. Families and children should see themselves and their communities reflected in the environment and materials. The physical environment represents the school's culture, climate, and values. Does the physical space address the needs of the families and the children served? For example, is the physical space modified and adapted to facilitate access and participation of families and/or children with disabilities (Catalino & Meyer 2016)? Strategically planned and well-maintained physical spaces offer opportunities to support diversity, belongingness, security, and collaboration. From the entrance lobby or front office, to the hallways, to the playground, the organization of the rooms, furnishings, equipment, and materials conveys messages about what the early learning program prioritizes.

Ways to Plan an Inclusive and Welcoming Space

- **Collaborate with families.** The DEC (2014) recommends collaborating with families to modify and adapt the environment to promote each child's access to and participation in learning experiences. Arranging the furniture and materials to ensure they are accessible to all children and families demonstrates a commitment to accessibility and equitable learning opportunities. For example, arrange furniture so children who use walkers can easily navigate the space or place materials on shelves so they can be reached by a child or a family member using a wheelchair.

- **Create a family resource center.** Create cozy, semi-private areas that encourage families to feel like part of the learning community, such as a family resource center. This space provides opportunities for families to collaborate and connect with the school leader, teachers, and/or other families and demonstrates a commitment to fostering open communication, participation, engagement, a sense of community, and belongingness. Continuously invite families and teachers to add to and change information and resources provided within the space, such as relevant magazines, lending library books, refreshments, and handouts about upcoming events. It can also serve as a take-and-exchange area where families can take or donate supplies and clothing. Invite all families into the space during drop-off and pickup.

- **Represent the whole school community.** Create spaces that allow for representation of the whole school community. For example, invite families to assist with creating displays or bulletin boards that represent the cultures, languages, traditions, and celebrations of the staff, families, and community. Showcase the displays throughout the learning environment (e.g., the lobby, office, and hallways). When appropriate and available, use actual photos from the learning community to feature the range of family structures (e.g., two moms, one-parent households, grandparents as primary caregivers). Such examples demonstrate a commitment to recognizing and accepting all families. Intentional curiosity and implementation demonstrate a commitment to uplifting, empowering, and celebrating diversity.

- **Use displays to communicate.** Clearly and creatively display the program's mission, the mascot, and pictures of staff. Label staff pictures with names, short bios, and their roles. Throughout the year, update the display so it stays current. For example, a private early childhood center invited employees to provide pictures and descriptions of vacations and events held in their classrooms. This helps families learn about all staff members.

- **Ask for feedback.** In the lobby and office, provide a place for feedback and suggestions. For example, an elementary school principal placed a decorated table in front of the office with a suggestion box, paper, and pens. To encourage families to use the suggestion box, you might implement a question of the month. The question serves as a prompt for families who might not know what to write as a suggestion.

Summary

All members of the learning community play roles in creating an inclusive and welcoming culture and climate. School leaders must recognize the importance of collaborating and connecting with key stakeholders and cultivate a team dynamic within the learning community. Leaders are tasked with dismantling barriers that prevent nondominant families from feeling a sense of belonging and safety within the school and classroom. They must clearly articulate decisions, policies, and practices and regularly co-evaluate them to prevent and break down barriers that encourage exclusion and marginalization. These leaders lay the foundation by demonstrating and modeling intentional reflection, active listening, and ongoing analysis. "Spaces need to be constructed in schools and communities where individuals from diverse backgrounds and abilities can express their concerns, share their experiences and ideas in their own words and forms of representation, engage in exploratory discussions, and negotiate multiple perspectives" (Lim & Renshaw 2001, 18). In such an environment, the climate is inviting, caring, and inclusive.

Reflect

1. In what ways does your early learning program's culture include and embrace the voices of families who speak a language other than English?

2. What messages does your school and classroom convey to families? How do you communicate those messages?

3. Developing trusting partnerships with families takes time and patience. It also requires dedication to reflecting on preconceived assumptions that lead to deficit mindset. Which communication methods and word choices do you use to reach out to and develop partnerships with families?

This chapter supports the following:

NAEYC Early Learning Program Accreditation Standards and Topic Areas

Standard 1: Relationships

1.D Creating a Predictable, Consistent, and Harmonious Classroom

Standard 3: Teaching

3.A Designing Enriched Learning Environments

Standard 9: Physical Environment

9.A Indoor and Outdoor Equipment, Materials, and Furnishings

Standard 10: Leadership and Management

10.B Management Policies and Procedures

Professional Standards and Competencies for Early Childhood Educators

Standard 4: Developmentally, Culturally, and Linguistically Appropriate Teaching Practices

4c: Use a broad repertoire of developmentally appropriate, culturally, and linguistically relevant, anti-bias, evidence-based teaching skills and strategies that reflect the principles of universal design for learning.

Hear Our Voices! Engaging in Partnerships that Honor Families

CHAPTER 4

Meeting the Needs of Families Through Assessment

Guiding Questions

As you read this chapter, consider the following:

1. What is your understanding of the relationship between assessments and reciprocal family partnerships?

2. In what ways does involving families in the assessment process support individualized development and learning for children and empowerment for families?

3. What strategies have you used to help families make sense of assessment practices and requirements?

FAMILY VOICES

It was crazy to get no answers [to my questions about curriculum], and I'm thinking, "I'm not trying to be a teacher, but since my daughter has Down syndrome, I want to know what we're working on and things that she's good at, that we don't need to stress about," and then talk about, "Okay, we should probably invest in these things." I had no help, nothing with respect to, "This is what we're doing." It really just seemed like, "Here's the gap in her development" and that's it. I'd think, "Whoa, show me in the spectrum of what you're doing because I want to talk about her strengths and use those for the gaps."

—White mother in a two-parent military family with three children, one of whom has a disability

The words *assessment* and *screening* can be intimidating to families. This is especially true for families who are unaware that there are many types of assessments conducted with young children for different purposes. A family member may think, "Why is my child being assessed? Is there a problem?," "Do I need to know about this?," or "I don't understand the words or explanations my child's teacher is using to discuss this assessment." Conversely, some families may ask, "Why isn't my child being screened? I see them struggling." When assessment is mentioned, families become anxious and just want answers and direction. In either situation, it is the educator's responsibility to help families understand the purpose of the assessment, show families how to interpret the results, and explain what strategies are appropriate to support their children's development and learning. Families are more confident in partnering with their children's early learning program and teachers when they understand the processes, outcomes, and applications of assessments. This chapter discusses the purposes of assessment and the types of assessments commonly used in early childhood settings, as well as the significant role families play in the assessment process, including Individualized Family Service Plan and Individualized Education Program discussions and planning.

Equity and the Assessment Process

The assessment process has historically been associated with systemic and institutional racism and injustices benefiting some children over others. For example, Black and Brown children are frequently underserved, overidentified for special education services, or denied access to gifted and advanced placement courses (Fritzgerald 2021; Hing 2014). As Rosales and Walker (2021) explain, "tests have been instruments of racism and a biased system. Decades of research demonstrate that Black, Latin(o/a/x), and Native students, as well as students from some Asian groups, experience bias from standardized tests administered from early childhood through college" (n.p.). More specifically, in early childhood settings, racial gaps and disparities in assessment processes, outcomes, access, and services begin early and extend into preschool and kindergarten (Allen et al. 2021; Aratani, Wight, & Cooper 2011; Sabol et al. 2021).

Preconceived assumptions, biases, and misinterpretations contribute to systemic injustices and inequitable opportunities, such as leaving some families out of the assessment process, and result in outcomes that impact children's development and achievement. Thus, "a critical step in the process is to reflect on and work against biases that may get in the way of assessing a child accurately and using the results from the assessment appropriately" (NAEYC 2022, 163). Examining personal biases and assessment practices and policies that privilege some children and families over others helps to address the inequities that persist within the educational system. For example, asking a child to compare and contrast two pictures of objects or places that the child is unfamiliar with or otherwise has no frame of reference for or conducting assessments solely in English with a child who speaks a different home language is inequitable and does not account for that child's experiences or cultural and linguistic background.

FAMILY VOICES

Everyone Is Unique

There's an expression: "If you've met one person with Down syndrome, you've met one person with Down syndrome."

—White mother in a two-parent military family with three children, one of whom has a disability

NAEYC (2022) outlines some steps to minimize the impact biases have on the assessment process, which include

1. Recognizing how one's own culture can affect expectations for children, the way children are assessed, and the judgements made based on assessment results

2. Focusing on documenting children's strengths rather than looking for ways they may demonstrate deficits or not meet expectations

3. Using multiple assessment strategies, including anecdotal observations and informal assessment tools so that children have multiple ways to demonstrate their competencies

4. Paying careful attention to whether the assessment tool has been shown to be reliable and valid for use with children who have similar characteristics to the children being assessed and, if not, being very cautious when interpreting and using results and to advocate for more appropriate practices (163)

Using a strengths-based approach and anti-bias education within the assessment process means viewing it through an equity lens and seeing each child as an individual, as well as considering contextual factors, such as the child's culture, home language, abilities, family structure, and development, in the analysis and decision-making process. In this approach, stakeholders continuously and collectively measure and evaluate the appropriateness and limitations of assessments.

Given what early childhood educators know about the value of assessments in informing curricular decisions, they must elevate and include the voices of families to assist with measuring the appropriateness, accuracy, and analysis of the assessments used within the learning setting. Such practices lead to more equitable outcomes by providing insight into the life of and many influences on the child. Involving families ensures all requirements and decisions are conducted in a transparent and collaborative manner and provides opportunities for families to advocate for their children, themselves, and others (Graybill & Easton 2015). Fostering reciprocal, transparent communication provides access for families who might be intimidated by the assessment process, reluctant to ask questions, or hesitant to engage due to language barriers. The Individuals with Disabilities Education Improvement Act (IDEA) of 2004 (Public Law 108-446) mandates that schools and families work together for children who receive special education services. This means that families must be equal and valuable members of the team to ensure the assessment process is authentic and strengths-based.

Looking to NAEYC Position Statements

Using assessments that meet families' needs is supported by

- "Advancing Equity in Early Childhood Education" position statement (NAEYC 2019)
  -) Recommendations for Early Childhood Educators
    - · Observe, Document, and Assess Children's Learning and Development, Item 2: Use authentic assessments that seek to identify children's strengths and provide a well-rounded picture of development.

- *Code of Ethical Conduct and Statement of Commitment* (NAEYC 2016)
  -) Section II: Ethical Responsibilities to Families
    - · Principle 2.7—We shall inform families about the nature and purpose of the program's child assessments and how data about their child will be used.

- "Developmentally Appropriate Practice" position statement (NAEYC 2020)
  -) Guideline 3: Observing, Documenting, and Assessing Children's Development and Learning, Item D: The methods of assessment are responsive to the current developmental accomplishments, language(s), and experiences of young children. They recognize individual variation in learners and allow children to demonstrate their competencies in different ways.

The following structures are key to promoting equitable assessment practices:

> **School leaders support the use of equitable and inclusive assessments.** They must know which assessments are used, how to conduct each assessment, the assessment requirements and expectations, and the process for analyzing the data obtained. School leaders must also ensure that steps are taken to actively involve families in the process. Part of this includes providing time and space beyond family-educator conferences for teachers and families to discuss and collaborate on requirements and outcomes.

> **Educators commit to equitable and inclusive assessment practices.** This includes recognizing and eliminating assessment practices that perpetuate stereotypes and biases and leave some children and families behind.

> **Educators continuously evaluate the accuracy and relevance of assessments.** This includes using various types of assessments (discussed in more detail later in this chapter) as well as collaborating with colleagues and families to analyze the assessments being used.

The Purposes of Assessment

Assessments are processes of gathering information related to a child's strengths, how a child learns, and what a child has learned to measure development and growth within the learning domains and specific content areas (Chen & McNamee 2007; Gonzalez-Mena 2012). Educators use assessments to get to know each child better. NAEYC (2020) explains that assessments determine where a child is compared to "the learning progressions that children typically follow, including the typical sequences in which skills and concepts develop" (26). Assessment data informs educators as they reflect on and make decisions about and changes to curricular, instructional, and environmental practices in order to meet the developmental, individual, cultural, and linguistic needs of a child. "In early intervention and early childhood special education, assessment is conducted for the purposes of screening, determining eligibility for services, individualized planning, monitoring child progress, and measuring child outcomes" (DEC 2014, 8).

Kostelnik and colleagues (2019) outline six reasons why educators assess children:

1. Inform instruction
2. Guide children's progress
3. Identify children who may benefit from special help or additional health services
4. Report children's progress to families
5. Assess strengths and limitations of your program of instruction
6. Hold yourself and your program accountable to funding and regulatory agencies, boards of directors, school boards, legislators, and citizen groups (210)

Early childhood educators conduct a variety of assessments of young children's development and learning throughout the year. These assessments can determine what a child knows and can do as well as the skills and knowledge they have mastered based on objectives, standards, and developmental expectations. Educators can use the data to develop individualized goals to meet the needs of each child. Furthermore, assessments measure the effectiveness of the teaching practices used within the early childhood classroom (NAEYC 2022).

Types of Assessment

Assessment in early childhood education can take many forms. For the purposes of this book, this chapter focuses on four types of assessment: formal, informal, summative, and formative.

Formal assessments are standardized, or regulated, processes or instruments that obtain information about a child's learning and development through specific—and often uniform—requirements (Bodrova & Leong 2018). Typically, this type of assessment is mandated and administered according to a schedule determined by the school, district, or state. Formal assessments measure children's accomplishments against the curricular standards and expectations set by the school, district, or state. Instruments such as the Phonological Awareness Literacy Screening (PALS) and the Dynamic Indicators of Basic Early Literacy

Skills (DIBELS) are examples of formal assessments used within the early childhood setting. Screenings are another type of formal assessment. They are "designed to identify children who may have significant developmental delays or disabilities" (Elicker & McMullen 2013, 24).

On the other hand, *informal assessments* are nonstandardized processes conducted in a child's natural setting on an ongoing basis. In this approach, educators use flexible methods of assessment that (1) let children demonstrate their strengths and (2) are responsive to and account for culturally and linguistically diverse backgrounds. Observations, portfolios, and anecdotal notes are examples of informal assessments. Assessments that fall under this category are often considered *authentic assessments* because they occur in a child's natural learning context (i.e., in a familiar educational setting with tasks that mirror a child's real-life, everyday experiences as closely as possible) and focus on discovering a child's best performance (Kostelnik et al. 2019). Families are an integral part of the process as they provide pertinent information on activities, routines, and settings the children partake in on a daily basis. Furthermore, this assessment approach is often conducted in a child's home language. NAEYC (2020) adds the following guidance:

> For children who speak a language the educators do not know, native speakers of the child's language such as family or community members may need to be recruited to assist with the assessment process. A plan should be in place for employing volunteer and paid interpreters and translators as needed and providing them with information about appropriate interactions with young children and ethics and confidentiality, as well as about the features and purposes of the screening or assessment tool. (20)

FAMILY VOICES

Early Diagnosis Is Important

My son was diagnosed very early, partly due to a lot of socioeconomic advantages that I have as a teacher with health care. I had a daycare provider who saw that he had signs of autism, and I was able to take him immediately to a pediatrician and get a referral to our local Department of Developmental Services. I've been told many times I've actually lucked out because there is only one referring psychiatrist at that facility, and I was able to get a slot and get him evaluated. He was formally diagnosed with autism spectrum disorder at 2 years old. The Department of Developmental Services did provide him with speech therapy services and an infant development specialist that came to our home. He was able to get that from ages 2 to 3. At age 3, he needed to go through the school district, where he was able to get speech services.

—White mother, early childhood educator and part of a single-parent family with one child who has a disability

Summative assessments are evaluations that take place at a specific point in time to determine if children have learned what is expected. They are almost always formal assessments. The results of these assessments for accountability purposes, to report on children's progress, or to compare learner performance.

Formative assessments are processes educators use to monitor children's learning. Educators use the data collected from formative assessments to modify teaching and learning activities to better serve children (Gillanders et al. 2021). These kinds of assessments are typically informal.

Educators must use all types of assessment throughout the year to understand the whole child, including their contexts, strengths, and needs. Moving flexibly among the various assessment types reduces the barriers that impact children's learning and development. To help make this feasible, educators can apply the principles of the universal design for learning. The *universal design for learning* (UDL) is a framework to optimize teaching and learning by "proactively designing curriculum and so the greatest number of students can benefit without the need for adaptations or changes" (Brillante 2017, 28). By tapping into the UDL principles, educators can make informed decisions when designing and reflecting on assessments by (CAST 2020)

> **Providing multiple means of engagement (the *why* of learning).** Do you use developmentally, individually, culturally, and linguistically appropriate assessments? Do you use formal, informal, formative, and summative assessments that meet the varying needs of the children served?

> **Providing multiple means of representation (the *what* of learning).** Do you consider the ways in which you present the assessments to the children? How do you explain the assessments to families?

> **Providing multiple means of action and expression (the *how* of learning).** Do you allow children to demonstrate their knowledge using multiple types of assessment? Do you use formal, informal, formative, and summative assessments for children to demonstrate their learning?

Connecting and Collaborating with Families on Assessment

Many families have a limited understanding of assessments, including expectations, regulations, processes, and how to interpret the outcomes. If they do have a perception about assessments, it is often formed from their personal experiences, such as being assessed while they were in school. No matter what degree of experience families have with assessments, they do have set goals and expectations for their children's development and growth, and they expect teachers and school leaders to facilitate these goals. For instance, the mother highlighted in the "Family Voices" feature on page 76 noted that her son, who was diagnosed with autism spectrum disorder at 2 years old, demonstrates strengths in math. When we dialogued, one thing she wanted her son's teachers to do was use his strengths in math to help with the areas he wasn't proficient in. She felt that an approach that focused on a skill at which her son excelled would help develop his self-esteem. Information and insights like this are integral to the

Listen to What Families Say They Need

The teachers wanted my son to be seen by a developmental pediatrician. They were really pushing a particular diagnosis on him. I was like, "I'm resistant until you talk to me about what's happening. Until we can speak to the things that he will be able to do at home and what he's not demonstrating at school and we talk about why, then I don't feel confident in your observation or your assessment." I end up pushing for my son to be assessed by the city because the city also has, if you were eligible for services, an early childhood intervention program. We go through the process with assessment and ultimately get the report, which says that your child can do all the things. Sensory processing integration stuff, yes, that's a challenge for him, but he's able to count to 15. He's able to do things that are developmentally appropriate and above. As far as needing support services at this time, he doesn't. Maybe in the future, there might be an additional need, and he can be reassessed at that time. Here are some strategies; here's some people that you should reach out to. What I appreciate about that whole process was how supportive they were. *That's* the kind of conversation that I wish I had gotten with the school.

—Latina mother in a two-parent family with two toddler-age children

assessment process and can be used to inform decision making and goal setting. NAEYC (2020) explains that "assessment focuses on children's progress toward developmental and educational goals. Such goals should reflect families' input as well as children's background knowledge and experiences" (20). It is important that "educators involve families as a source of information about the child (before program entry and on an ongoing basis), and they engage families in the planning for their child, including teaching practices, curriculum planning and implementation, and assessments" (NAEYC 2020, 18). Partnering with families on assessment requires learning about each family; meeting with families to explain and discuss the assessments being used; and collaborating with families on their child's growth, development, and learning strengths and needs. Educators should inform families about the assessments their children are required to take, when they will receive the results, and how to interpret the results. However, beyond these essentials, families have the right to more fully understand these assessments. Think about the tests administered in your school, district, and state. How many of the families you serve understand the why and how of these assessments?

When families receive relevant information about their children and the assessments used within the classroom, they gain understanding of the processes, outcomes, and application of assessments. In return, families are more empowered and confident in their role within the assessment process and are more willing to become active partners with their children's teachers. Providing families with multiple opportunities to review copies of various assessment tools can go a long way in helping them understand how and why those assessments are used.

Typically, families learn about state testing during the month that it will be administered with little explanation beyond the basics (e.g., the what and when). Instead, during the initial visit or meeting with each family at the start of the school year, educators can take the time to explain the assessments children will undergo. Waiting until family-educator conferences or when the test is about to be administered to make the initial contact with families limits the chances of connection as well as didactic learning and goal setting related to the child. Learning about assessment processes—and especially assessment results—for the first time in either of these scenarios can be jarring and frustrating for families. I can recall my daughter's teacher waiting until the family-educator conference in November to discuss the challenges my daughter was having in math content. Had the teacher informed me earlier in the academic year, I would have collaborated with her to ensure my child mastered the content.

Allow families to discuss their concerns, goals, and any other questions they might have. This is also a time to clearly define key terms, explain any educational jargon, and spell out any acronyms (e.g., what PALS stands for and why is it used). When assessment results are sent home, families are often asked to sign and return a form confirming that they have received and read the results. This sometimes includes an invitation to email the teacher if they have questions regarding the assessment results; however, a family might not know what questions to ask because they do not understand how to read or interpret the assessment results. Remember to make information available in the format (e.g., in-person meeting, email, print handouts) and language most helpful for each family.

Common Questions Families Have About Assessment

- What is assessment? What is this specific assessment?

- What is the assessment process? What is my child expected to do? What is the format (e.g., pencil and paper, oral, computer)?

- Why is my child being assessed?

- What is being measured?

- Is this assessment something all the children will participate in? Is it required?

- When will the assessment take place? Will my child be pulled out of class and miss instructional time?

- Are the assessments graded or scored?

- How are the results used? How do I interpret the results sent home?

- What is my role as a family member in this process?

The following list outlines tips for working and communicating with families about assessment:

> **Be intentional.** Initiate ongoing dialogue with each child's family. Keep a family communication logbook. Each time you dialogue with families, keep track of the date and timeline, topic, outcome, and next steps. Make sure to follow through with the timeline and follow up with families throughout the year to provide updates and ask for feedback.

> **Clearly communicate basic information about assessments.** What assessments do you use throughout the school year, and when will you administer them? What is the purpose of these assessments? What do they measure? How are these things measured? How is the collected data analyzed? Who is involved in the assessment process, and what are their roles and responsibilities?

> **Create an assessment calendar.** Use the calendar to help plan and schedule appropriate times to discuss and explain assessments. Conduct check-in calls to ensure families understand how to interpret the results of the assessments. This is particularly important for formal assessments.

> **Provide information continually.** Communicating about assessment is not a one-and-done proposition. Prior to conducting assessments, send information home via a short and simple handout or create a short video explaining the assessment and how to interpret the results.

> **Discuss results with families together.** After conducting the assessment, provide opportunities to dialogue with individual families about their child's results, the process for reading the results, and next steps (e.g., collaborating to set and meet goals). Assist families with understanding and interpreting the results from the assessment.

Table 4.1 on page 81 provides an overview of a few additional dos and don'ts for how to communicate effectively during family-educator conferences.

The Assessment Team

As discussed in Chapter 3, team building is important to creating a positive learning community and environment. Teams in general can provide additional supports and present more opportunities to address issues, answer questions, and solve problems. "Collaborating with colleagues around [. . .] assessment topics, collecting and analyzing data, discussing outcomes, examining challenges, and recommending solutions can be both effective and empowering" (CAST 2020, 5). Likewise, the assessment team is a group of individuals who bring expertise to the assessment process to gain a more detailed understanding of the child and to decide on what's best for their development and learning.

Table 4.1. Dos and Don'ts for Effective Communication During Family-Educator Conferences

Do . . .	Don't . . .
Discuss progress, goals, and an action plan	Compare a child or their performance to other children
Display portfolios and documentation boards of each child's work	Expect families to understand how to interpret the portfolio or the documentation boards without guidance
Ask families for input about their child's strengths, needs, interests, and experiences	Psychoanalyze the family in an attempt to determine the causes for the child's needs or challenging behaviors
Collaborate with families to determine how best to include knowledge gained about the family (e.g., traditions, activities) in the assessment approaches	Assume that a family does not bring value to the classroom
Ensure translators are available as needed and translate materials and resources in a family's preferred language	Argue with or blame families for their lack of understanding
Keep in mind goals and accommodations for children with an Individualized Family Service Plan, Individualized Education Program, or 504 plan, and collaborate with the specialist to ensure goals are met	Use educational jargon and expect families to agree to recommendations with little to no explanation or dialogue
Focus on the strengths of the child and use those strengths to develop concrete strategies to ensure the child meets set goals	Focus on what a child cannot do
Be objective when communicating assessment data	Communicate using words that are intensifiers or absolutes (e.g., *very, really, always, never*)

The assessment team should consist of anyone who is invested in the child: the child's family, the lead teacher, the instructional assistant, the school leader, the school counselor or psychologist, any specialists who work with the child, and sometimes an interpreter. This team might change and should remain flexible depending on the child and their needs. Building a team is grounded in anti-bias education and a strengths-based approach, and the team's purpose is forming a community that collectively sets goals, aligns practices, and evaluates assessment outcomes to devise decisions and goals based on data collected. Developed at the start of the school year, the team focuses on being proactive instead of reactive. The team identifies strategies and establishes timelines for goals that are set.

Forming relationships that are built on trust is paramount to the success of the team and the development of the child. Educators can build bridges between the child's home and the early learning program if they view assessment as an ongoing process that requires input, insight, and shared goals from all key stakeholders. It is imperative that the team continuously and consistently collaborate to reflect on what is and is not working to promote the development and learning of each child. This requires intentional planning to create various opportunities for reciprocal dialogues about the child's development, progress, and needs. It also involves strategies that will promote equitable learning opportunities, such as conducting regular check-in sessions with families to discuss progress.

FAMILY VOICES

A Team Effort

Last year, I noticed that our son was having a lot of issues coping with his feelings that seemed to occur most frequently after visitation with his father. This carried out through fights with other kids at school, more aggressiveness in the classroom, and it started to escalate. It ended up being initially maybe a little disagreement, and then it escalated into fighting with other students. This led to my son receiving an in-school suspension, which has never happened. He's in second grade, this has never happened to him. I was actually very surprised something was really bothering him.

I was able to continue therapy sessions—we go to a family therapist now to deal with the emotions, the feelings that he has during the transition [between two different homes in the middle of the week, every week], and also with the co-parenting aspect with my ex-husband because there are very different parenting styles between the two homes. Our son was acting this out in school, because he didn't know how to deal with his feelings about these changes. I reached out to the counselor through the teacher and asked that if there was a way for the counselor to meet with my son the mornings after he had visitation with his dad, to give him an opportunity to calm any anxieties, or any sadness, or any issues, maybe catch him in the morning and sit down with him and have a conversation with him to help him start the day positively. Then we started to document when these behavioral changes would occur, the frequency of them, when she would meet and talk with him. This got the teacher, the counselor, and our family therapist all sharing information to help my son to perform his best at school. It also helped at home.

—Black mother who is a single parent with one child

Personal Connection Is an Important Foundation

I really like my older daughter's teacher. She quickly identified some areas of growth for my daughter and was very transparent with me. Since then, we've set a schedule to improve those areas and talk about how it's going. This teacher is also skilled at understanding that her role is first to connect with the student and understand what drives the student. What I think connects teachers to their students is that they also understand how important it is to understand people.

—Mother of a family with four children

Individualized Family Service Plan and Individualized Education Program Meetings

"Early childhood educators participate as professional partners in Individualized Family Service Plan (IFSP) teams for children birth to 3 and in Individualized Education Program (IEP) teams for children ages 3 through 8" (NAEYC 2021, 46). Families are critical team members in the IFSP and IEP processes. An IFSP outlines the early intervention services provided to a young child and their family (Brillante 2017). An IEP lays out the special education instruction, supports, and services a child needs to thrive in school (Baumel 2022). According to IDEA, families are first on the list of required members of a child's IEP team (Belsky, n.d.), which clearly recognizes families as the most important members of the process.

In spite of this, many nondominant families who attend IFSP and IEP meetings feel isolated, alone, uneducated, anxious, and lost because of the jargon and terminology used (Peterson 2019; Reiman et al. 2010). This is especially true for families whose primary language is not English if there are no interpreters present or translated materials prepared. Furthermore, when goals are set for the child with little input from the families, families develop a lack of trust for the process and all parties involved. Negative experiences families encounter during IFSP and IEP meetings can deter them from seeking the input they need to navigate and understand the process, which impacts their children. Families have reported feeling as though their primary role is to listen or answer questions and agree with goals and placements already decided by school staff; they often feel overwhelmed by the pace of the meeting and educational jargon (Childre & Chambers 2005; Mueller & Buckley 2014).

Understanding Is Key

My son has an IEP for speech. That process was long, and I didn't know the timelines for how that all works. The IEP process was difficult, even with my background with schools. It's different from county to county, state to state.

—Asian mother in a two-parent military family with two children

• • • • • •

Harrison (Black father, part of a blended two-parent family with three children): That was the word I was looking for. They wanted to put him on IEP. For me back then, my ignorance was that I thought an IEP meant that there was something wrong with my son. I automatically thought there was a stigma they were trying to put on my son because he was a Black child. The teachers and administrators really sat down with me, explained the situation and said, "This is something that he can work his way out of, but he just needs that additional support." We have a one-to-one therapist for him, and as he improves, those services will decrease. My son did have an IEP for his first year and a half of early childhood. He went to private school for pre-K. Then in kindergarten and first grade, he had his IEP and his occupational therapist.

Bweikia Steen: The occupational therapist—what did they do to help ease your fears? It sounds like you had fears related to the IEP, especially knowing the research for Black boys. How did they ease your fears?

Harrison: Of course, I went to the furthest end of the spectrum. I thought they were going to put my son on medication and all kinds of stuff. Some of the horror stories that I've heard, some of the things that I had seen, because I too worked in education for a brief period in DC. I worked for a school with . . . they called them emotionally disturbed and socially maladjusted African American young men. I saw some of the IEPs and I saw the behaviors of some of those children, and that was all I could think about. I expressed that to the staff at the school. They sat down with me for a very long time and explained to me everything in full detail, that this was something that would be beneficial to him. They didn't see him being in for a long period of time or an extended period of time. It really eased my fears. They gave me the entire manual, all the things that they were going to do. They introduced me to the occupational therapist. They really laid it out for me.

Here are some quick tips for collaboratively approaching the IFSP and IEP processes and promoting trust:

> Introduce the entire IFSP or IEP team. State each team member's name and role in the process. Invite family members to introduce themselves.

> Discuss and explain key terms.

> Remain open and inclusive to all perspectives.

> Periodically stop throughout the process to check in on the family and to solicit their input (e.g., "What are you seeing at home?," "What does your child like to play with their siblings?").

> Collectively agree on the goals and action items.

> Develop a timeline to check in on the progress toward accomplishing the goals. Set check-in dates to follow up on the child's progress.

> Conduct monthly check-ins with the families to dialogue about the goals that were set and the instructional strategies that were agreed on. Use a logbook to document each check-in.

> Reflect on the set goals and the various assessments used to measure whether the goals were met.

Providing Adequate Resources for Children with IEPs

One inequity I see for my son, for students I've had in my class, and students I see around my campus is that the public school system often needs to find ways to accommodate IEPs and yet fit their budget and their own ideas of how to spend their district money. What I've noticed is that, oftentimes, if there was more than one inclusion student on a school site, they will cluster them into a single class so that they may split their teacher's aide. Technically, the students have a full-time aide in their class, but it's not really a full-time, one-on-one aide for each student.

My son was never required to have a one-on-one aide—it just said that he had to have aide time. Legally, this did fit his IEP. In second grade, he was included with another child that needed an aide in his class. The aide was very, very much needed for the other child, so my child did not get a lot of aide time that year. Even though the aide was in the class with him, he did not get the aide time that he was supposed to get according to his IEP. Legally, it probably fit because the aide was there in the room with him as was required. However, for the actual day-to-day management of activities, the aide was far more focused on the other child, as was needed. For my child, this ended up being fine because, as I've mentioned, I have full communication with the teachers. I am a teacher. I have ways to intervene with him at home, and I have a support system. For other parents who don't understand the educational system, don't have full access to the teachers, or don't know that their child's aide is actually being shared with other students in the class, I could see how this could be a big inequity for those families and those students.

—White mother, early childhood educator and part of a
single-parent family with one child who has a disability

Summary

Families are the experts on their children, and their knowledge is valuable for informing decisions related to assessment. Using a strengths-based approach and anti-bias education recognizes the value in partnering with families across all aspects of the assessment process. Demystifying the assessment process for families—what types of assessment are used, why they are used, and how the results are analyzed and used—helps to eliminate barriers that prevent them from collaborating with their children's teachers. With a joint clear and concise understanding of assessments, all stakeholders work together to meet the needs of each child. When families are seen as valuable partners within the assessment process, trust is built. This collaboration is an investment in each child's development and learning.

Reflect

1. Think about the guiding questions posed at the beginning of the chapter. After reading this chapter, what other assessment strategies could you implement to promote reciprocal family partnerships?

2. Which types of assessment are conducted in your classroom? When you connect with families to discuss assessment, what types of conversations do you have (e.g., explanatory, investigatory, collaborative)?

This chapter supports the following:

NAEYC Early Learning Program Accreditation Standards and Topic Areas

Standard 4: Assessment of Child Progress

4.C Identifying Children's Interests and Needs and Describing Children's Progress

4.E Communicating with Families and Involving Families in the Assessment Process

Professional Standards and Competencies for Early Childhood Educators

Standard 3: Child Observation, Documentation, and Assessment

3c: Use screening and assessment tools in ways that are ethically grounded and developmentally, ability, culturally, and linguistically appropriate in order to document developmental progress and promote positive outcomes for each child.

3d: Build assessment partnerships with families and professional colleagues.

CHAPTER 5

Strategies and Activities for Honoring and Partnering with Families

Reflect: Putting It Together

After you read all the chapters, consider the following:

1. In what ways does honoring families promote reciprocal family partnerships?

2. Think about the connections you've made with families. What strategies have you used to invite families into dialogue about their goals, questions, and concerns?

3. True dialogue empowers all stakeholders to collectively develop shared goals. What does empowerment mean to you in relation to reciprocal family partnerships?

FAMILY VOICES

My goal for my son is that he loves school. I see elementary school—school period, really—as an extension of the village it takes to raise these children. For me, school is part of that village. I want my son to know that that village cares about him. That he is loved and valued. That they see past the behavior. Children cut up, they do—and it's not to excuse, I'll deal with the bad behavior—but that's what they do. I want his teachers to use the power of their words and influence to strengthen him and to build him up. Go past what you're seeing on the outside. Yeah, he talks too much, he talks too much at home, but go past that and see he is bright and he is intelligent and he is full of curiosity—and feed that.

I think we just got to do better. We've got to use the power of our words, again, to uplift and inspire and encourage. It's important. We are the nurturers, as parents, as teachers, as influencers, and it's a powerful position to be in. We've got to do better with that power. Thank you for allowing me to share my story. I am encouraged, and I appreciate what you all are doing.

—Black mother in a single-parent family with a 5-year-old child

What Does It Mean to Honor Families?

> Through dialogue, people come together and participate in all crucial aspects of investigation and collective action. This cannot be achieved through the exercise of merely answering questions in a conventional questionnaire or a formalized interview, because these techniques do not allow the respondent to speak in a full voice. (Park et al. 1993, 12)

Families leave their children in the hands of early learning programs with the expectation of those programs providing a safe, welcoming environment that fosters the development and learning of their children. Furthermore, families expect that the educators in those programs will embrace them as partners and acknowledge, as Maguire (1987) says, that "we both know some things, neither of us knows everything, working together we will both know more, and we will both learn more about how to know" (39). When school leaders and teachers honor the families they serve, they understand that advancing equitable partnerships among all families begins when they dialogue with families. Wink (2005) refers to dialogue as "change agent chatter" (41). In other words, dialogue empowers all key stakeholders to tap into the strengths gained from lived experiences. It informs decision making regarding the children, the early learning program, and the structures and processes that impact the children and families the program serves. By providing space and opportunities for families to express their opinions and concerns about their children's learning experiences, educators can learn from what families have to say, reflect on that knowledge, and use it to improve on their practice.

When I became a parent, I experienced firsthand some of what these families had dialogued with me about for years, including implicit biases, a deficit mindset, and educators who did not understand the importance of partnership. I still remember dropping my 3-year-old daughter off on her first day of preschool. At the time, she attended a very affluent early learning program with a high-quality curriculum and an outstanding reputation. I was so excited about what she was going to learn that year, and she was overjoyed to be a big girl. As the weeks passed, I noticed that her jubilant spirit began to decline. By the third week, the school leader approached me with a concern from my daughter's teacher. She stated that my daughter needed occupational and physical therapy. When I asked why, she replied that my daughter had fallen out of her seat. I then further inquired, "How many times has she fallen out of her seat?" She responded, "Once." I was dismayed that the school leader and the teacher decided that my daughter required services due to one incident without consulting or involving me in the decision-making process. This conversation set the tone for my family's relationship with the educators at the program moving forward.

The dreams I had for my daughter's first year of preschool slowly faded as I witnessed repeated inequitable judgments and expectations for her. The trust and excitement that I initially felt dissipated, replaced by fear, hurt, disappointment, and anger. Suddenly, I found myself in the shoes of so many families I had spoken to over the years—needing advocates and searching for a team of like-minded professionals, family members, and friends who understood my child and our story. I looked for anyone who would be willing to help me navigate my child's educational experiences. I wanted to ensure decisions and strategies would further my child's success, both academically and beyond. Assistance and reassurance did come from teachers, instructional assistants, after-school program staff, and a colleague who saw my daughter's strengths. These intentional educators invested in learning about my family and my child's experiences and needs. Because of my knowledge as an educator and my personal experiences, I knew who to approach, who to involve, and who I needed on my team. However, many diverse families do not know how to navigate the education system or that they can and should use their voices to influence decisions made about their child's education. My personal experiences confirmed the research I was conducting and my belief that every family is a valued member of the early learning team with shared goals for each child's success.

A child's home is their first classroom, and their family members are their first and most essential teachers (Banks & McGee Banks 2005; Berns 2004; Clark 1983; Delpit 2006). As Kohl (1994) states, education works best when "it merges the skills and knowledge of the community with the skills and knowledge of the educator" (62). Every family has a story, a history, experiences, and circumstances that influence their behavior, involvement, and engagement. When educators take the time to listen to and learn from the families they serve, children succeed and thrive.

Honoring each child's family means reflecting on biases, initiating and maintaining trusting connections, embracing individuality, and using flexible approaches and varied modes of engagement to build reciprocal family partnerships. Embracing anti-bias education and a strengths-based approach affects how educators view and partner with each child's family. Early childhood educators cannot let biased impressions and assumptions convince them that specific families do not care or are unreachable. It is their role to rewrite the narrative by rethinking reciprocal family partnerships and disrupting the policies and practices that leave out some families. Honoring families does not mean expecting families to fit a preconceived norm of what partnerships should look and feel like.

Although you should look for similarities that can connect you to the families you serve, do not allow differences to serve as barriers. Instead, learn more about those differences and embrace the diversity. *Differences* in a family's approach to partnering with the early learning program do not mean *disinterest*. Foster relationships that are based on shared goals and decision making to promote a sense of belonging for all families. Most importantly, place child learning and well-being as top priorities, recognizing reciprocal family partnerships as foundational to supporting whole child development

The sections that follow highlight key points from each chapter as well as practical strategies and activities that tie into those ideas. Strategies geared more toward teachers are indicated by this icon, whereas those for school leaders are indicated by this icon . Some of the suggestions are for both teachers and school leaders.

Chapter-by-Chapter Review, Strategies, and Activities

Chapter 1: Why Family Voices and Their Stories Matter

Key Chapter Points

1. The definition of *family* is broad and embraces diverse family structures.

2. Educators who understand that families are their children's first teachers know that understanding and effectively supporting children begins by dialoguing with their families. They respect the voices and perspectives of families as collaborators in the development and learning of the children.

3. All educators enter their classrooms with their own norms, biases, and expectations based on home experiences, cultures, and personal and professional experiences with the learning environment. These norms and biases can impede an educator's ability to develop positive relationships with each child's family.

4. Intentional dialogue and active listening with families can initiate reflection on biases and inequitable processes and lead to action.

FAMILY VOICES

It's About More than Just Academics

Minerva (Black mother in a two-parent family with two children): [Our goal] around education is just helping our children to navigate the entire school system. When they're learning in school, we want to complement it with an African American perspective, specifically history. That's definitely a goal for us, so that our children are . . . what would be the word?

Yuusuf (Black father in a two-parent family with two children): Well-rounded.

Minerva: Well-rounded. High self-esteem is one of the reasons why we decided to put them in the public school that they're in now. It's a diverse school—not necessarily the staff, but the children are diverse and giving them that experience.

Yuusuf: We didn't want our kids to be the only ones in the classroom. We wanted them to be around kids who look like them.

Minerva: Well-roundedness is important to us. Then, I think also just helping our kids to find their purpose in life and to become well-rounded adults eventually.

Strategies and Activities

1. **Family Philosophy Statement.** Create a statement that describes your reciprocal family partnership philosophy. Make sure it

   - Considers how Bronfenbrenner's ecological systems theory can inform your family philosophy

   - Indicates one strategy you would use to ensure each family has a voice within the early learning program and classroom environment

2. **Ask Families.** Send a brief survey to families to gauge their availability and preferences in partnering with their child's early learning program. See Table 5.1 for an example.

Table 5.1. Availability Survey

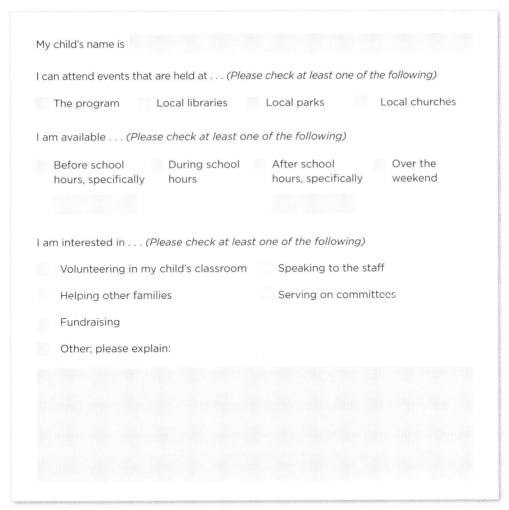

My child's name is

I can attend events that are held at . . . *(Please check at least one of the following)*

- The program
- Local libraries
- Local parks
- Local churches

I am available . . . *(Please check at least one of the following)*

- Before school hours, specifically
- During school hours
- After school hours, specifically
- Over the weekend

I am interested in . . . *(Please check at least one of the following)*

- Volunteering in my child's classroom
- Speaking to the staff
- Helping other families
- Serving on committees
- Fundraising
- Other; please explain:

Chapter 2: Building Reciprocal Family Partnerships

Key Chapter Points

1. Reciprocal family partnerships build on the positive foundations of participation, involvement, and engagement to create ongoing, supportive, and two-way collaboration between educators (both school leaders and teachers) and families. Partnerships are an essential part of the learning community and whole child development.

2. Families of color and diverse families have historically been expected to attend early learning program events, reach out to school leaders and teachers, and accept the advice and suggestions from educators without being afforded opportunities to provide their own input.

3. Systemic injustices and institutional racism disproportionately impact practices and outcomes for diverse children and their families. They place barriers to learning and establishing trusting reciprocal family partnerships.

4. A school leader who has committed to including anti-bias education within the program's mission and vision is committed to reflecting on the role of implicit biases in decision making. They embody an openness to learning from children's families and acknowledge that families are at the heart of the early childhood program. In this way, they ensure equitable opportunities for learning and development for each child and their family (Alanís & Iruka with Friedman 2021).

FAMILY VOICES

Laying Out Goals

I hope for my son to continue to succeed in school academically; have good behavior; get along with his peers; respect and listen to his teacher, his classmates, and administrators in the school; and just continue to do well in school.

—Black mother in single-parent family with one child

Strategies and Activities

1. **Mission and Vision Statements (Part 1).** Analyze your early learning program's mission and vision statements to make sure they meet the needs of everyone in the learning community. Consider the following questions:

   - When was the last time the program reviewed the mission and vision statements? Is it time to revise or update these statements in any way?

   - Do families know the program's vision and mission?

   - Is the program's vision and mission inclusive of all young children and their families?

2. **Mission and Vision Statements (Part 2).** Evaluate how your current early learning program's mission and/or vision statement relates to developing reciprocal family partnerships. Here are some steps you might take to begin the process:

   - Invite all stakeholders to engage in evaluating the current mission and/or vision statement. Determine which stakeholders are involved for each step.

   - Create and share goals (e.g., making the development of reciprocal family partnerships a priority), steps (e.g., sending out surveys, evaluating feedback), and a timeline for the evaluation and revision of the statement.

   - Consider key questions, such as whether the process ensures equitable opportunities for all families to provide feedback.

   - Use various communication strategies to solicit feedback about potential changes and revisions, including newsletters, in-person events (e.g., family-educator conferences), and surveys and polls conducted in print and digital formats (e.g., bulletin boards, Instagram, TikTok).

   - Evaluate the feedback.

   - Revise the statement based on recommendations from stakeholders.

   - Review changes with stakeholders.

   - Implement the revised statement with the early learning community.

3. **Policies and Procedures.** Review your early learning program's or school district's policies and procedures related to family partnership.

   - Talk with your colleagues about which families and populations you feel are left out or hindered by these policies and procedures.

   - Invite families, particularly those you identified as being previously excluded from the conversation, to develop new program-wide goals and measurable outcomes that will reduce inequities and improve engagement for all families.

4. **Family Questionnaire.** Choose one family in your class and create an individualized questionnaire for them to complete so that you can gain a better understanding of who they are as a family. The following are sample questions you might include in the questionnaire:

Basic Identifying and Demographic Questions

- What is your child's name and preferred name (nickname)?
- What are the names of your child's family members (including siblings and their ages)?

Child-Specific Questions

- What are your child's hobbies and interests (e.g., toys, games, people, and experiences)?
- What is your child's favorite thing to do?
- Does your child have a favorite toy? If yes, what is it?
- Does your child have a favorite food? If yes, what is it?
- Does your child have any pets? If yes, indicate what kind of animal(s) and their name(s).

Family-Specific Questions

- What language(s) are spoken at home?
- In what language do you prefer to communicate with me?
- Does your family have any traditions you would like me to be aware of?
- If you're comfortable sharing, identify your family's religion and if there are events or activities that you prefer your child not participate in.
- Is there anything else you want me to know?

5. **Home Visits.** Choose one family in your class and schedule a home visit with them at a mutually convenient time. Dialogue with the family, asking questions about their expectations for you as their child's teacher and their child's education experience in general. Some questions you might ask include

- What characteristics do you look for in a teacher?
- What do you need from your child's teacher to help you build trust and safety?
- What is your preferred method of communication with your child's teacher?
- Tell me about your child's favorite toy or hobby.
- Tell me about your child's favorite thing to talk about.

6. **Photographs and Videos.** Send families photos and videos of their children engaging in various activities in the classroom to more effectively communicate and connect what their children are learning. For infants and toddlers, this might be done daily, while for preschoolers, kindergartners, and primary grade children this can be done less frequently (a few times a week). Give context for the photos and videos shared, such as the time of day and a brief comment to describe what is happening. Table 5.2 shows how you might format this information.

Table 5.2. Sharing Photos

Child's name: Oluwande

Time of Day	Picture and/or Video	Teacher Comments
Morning Meeting		Oluwande is intently focused as we go over the schedule for the day.
Math		He explored extending and creating patterns with art materials, including paint.
Science		While in the community garden, Oluwande and his classmates learned about what plants need to grow and thrive.

7. **Introductory Video.** Use a video creation website or app (e.g., Animoto, Simpleshow, TikTok) to introduce yourself to children's families. Create a minute-long video that includes

   - Your name

   - Your hometown

   - How long you have been an educator

   - Your hobbies

   - Your philosophy on family partnerships

   Be creative! Creating short videos is fun and easy to do. They are simple to share via email or text. Families can even respond by creating a video of their own.

8. **Books and Photo Albums.** Create a book or album of photos to share with families periodically (e.g., at the end of each quarter). Websites, such as Book Creator (www.bookcreator.com), and apps can help you create these albums.

9. **Family Webpage.** Create a program or classroom webpage with interactive capabilities (e.g., families can watch videos of their children participating in class, children and families can post blogs). Some helpful websites for creating webpages include Google Classroom, Odoo, SimpleSite, Wix, and WordPress. At the beginning of the school year, send a survey asking families what they want you to include on your webpage. Provide a suggested list of items and at least one open-ended response (e.g., information about the teacher, classroom, staff, or early learning program; information about the schedule; information about the curriculum and expectations).

Chapter 3: Creating a Caring Community and Welcoming Environment

Key Chapter Points

1. The early childhood program community functions best as a team in which each member knows they are part of that community and is seen as a key stakeholder in the success of the program and children.

2. A program's culture is evident in the way in which its school leader, teachers, and staff communicate with families, each other, and the community.

3. Communication in any form, conscious and unconscious, can impact families' sense of safety and belonging.

4. Using a strengths-based approach, educators acknowledge that there are barriers that prevent many families from participating in the program. They strive to make engagement opportunities more accessible by being receptive and responsive to families' feedback about their needs. Some barriers are more obvious, whereas others are more intangible, such as when a family feels mistrustful because they have been marginalized or ignored due to implicit biases.

5. The physical environment plays a significant role in welcoming families and visually represents the program's culture, climate, and values. The physical space must address the needs of the families and the children served.

Strategies and Activities

1. **School Team.** Identify the members of your early learning team. Then, consider the following to ensure this team is inclusive and has a clear purpose:

    -   What are the team's goals?

    -   Why should the members who you identified be part of this team?

    -   Are the team members you identified representative of the early learning program's culture?

    -   How often will this team meet?

2. **Highlight the Staff.** Create a directory that includes the following information for each staff member:

    -   Name and a recent photo

    -   A brief (3–4 sentences) bio

    -   Their role (e.g., for a teacher, what grade they teach and how many years they've been teaching)

    -   Goals for the school year

    -   Hobbies

    Share the directory with families in multiple ways (e.g., posting it on the program webpage, sending printouts home, posting it on a bulletin board in the main office). Remember to update the directory periodically.

3. **Family Surveys.** Survey families throughout the year to keep current on their needs, wants, and feelings about the early learning program. You can ask open-ended questions and prompts like the following:

    -   What do you feel is working at the program for your child?

    -   I need my child's early learning program to . . .

    Provide the survey using different formats (e.g., online, text message, printouts posted in the hallways).

4. **Welcome Postcards.** Before the school year begins, mail postcards with brief notes to welcome children and their families to your classroom. See Figure 5.1 for an example. Although postcards may seem outdated, children and families like to receive them.

Figure 5.1. Postcard

Dear Vico,

I'm so excited to have you in my class this year! I can't wait to meet you and your family during our home visit on August 31 at 1:00 p.m. What are you most looking forward to this year?

I'll see you soon!
Mr. Edwards

5. **Preferred Communication Questionnaire.** Send a brief survey, like the example in Table 5.3, to families to inquire about how they prefer to receive and send communications.

Table 5.3. Communication Questionnaire

My child's name is

I would like to communicate with my child's teacher . . .

☐ Every day ☐ Every week ☐ Every month ☐ As needed ☐ No preference

My preferred method of communication is . . . *(Please check one of the following)*

☐ Text messages, and the best number to reach me is

☐ Email, and my preferred email address is

☐ Phone calls, and the best number to reach me is

☐ Zoom

☐ Other; please explain:

6. **Frequent and Positive Communication.** Share brief, positive messages with families. Each method can happen weekly for the first six weeks of school, then monthly for the remainder of the school year. Reaching out to families in fun, informal ways builds connections between you and families and helps families feel more comfortable reaching out to you. Add to this list of suggestions as you become more confident in reaching out to families. (*Note:* Keep in mind that privacy and security are critical. Do not post or text any information that is sensitive or could be misrepresented.)

   • **Method 1: Text messages.** Send families a one-sentence text with a photo or two of their children participating in an activity. (*Example: Here's a picture of Djimon cutting strips of paper to make a rainbow during free play today!*)

   • **Method 2: Video messages.** Send a short (less than one minute) video message via email or text. When possible, include the child in the video message. (*Example: Hi, Mrs. J! Jessica and I wanted to let you know that we are at recess playing on the swings. Have a great day!*)

7. **Nonverbal Communication.** Review Figure 5.2. With a colleague, practice communicating positive messages to families, focusing on each element of nonverbal communication (i.e., facial expression, eye contact, posture, hands, distance).

Figure 5.2. The Importance of Nonverbal Communication for Teachers and School Leaders

How educators stand and look when engaging with families conveys a message. Nonverbal communication is equally as important as verbal communication. Nonverbal communication sends messages to families about safety, belonging, and respect. Here are some elements of nonverbal communication to consider.

Facial expression. Reflect on how your thoughts and feelings show on your face. Recognize how a smile, a frown, or eyebrow movements play a role in perception.

Eye contact. Maintain a steady gaze as a sign of respect. Remain aware of eyerolling or side-eyeing.

Posture. An open posture communicates interest and readiness to listen. Face the person you are speaking with, keep your hands apart, and lean in instead of away.

Hands. Keep your hands apart to contribute to an open posture. Crossed arms contribute to a closed posture, which can imply a lack of comfort or interest, disagreement, or defensiveness.

Distance. How far you stand from someone reflects the level of your relationship. Standing too close can make a person uncomfortable, especially if you don't know them very well.

Adapted from a visualization created by Gina Tomko and *Education Week*, informed by Ruby Nadler, PhD, leadership consultant; SIGMA Assessment Systems, Inc.; and *Education Week* reporting, for A.M. Bichu, "7 Ways School Leaders Can Master Nonverbal Communication," *Education Week* (September/October 2022).

8. **Language Translators.** Advocate for language translators to be present within the learning community. Translators can assist with both oral and written communication among families, children, and educators. Make sure all stakeholders—but especially families—are made aware that translators and their services are available.

9. **Technology Tools for Communication.** Explore using technology developed to facilitate and streamline two-way dialogue between educators and families. Some platforms you might consider include TalkingPoints and ParentSquare.

10. **Rethink Open House and Back-to-School Nights.** Reimagine how you can make these staple events more accessible and engaging for families. Ask families for their input and ideas. For example, you might

    - Hold these events using a hybrid format. Also, send the meeting materials (e.g., handouts, slides, video clips) to all families within 24 hours after the event.

    - Include interactive activities, like a scavenger hunt. Ask families to find places and objects around the classroom and building (e.g., their child's desk, the dramatic play area, the library, the cafeteria). As families find each item on the list, provide information—either with fliers posted to share details or staff members strategically placed to engage in conversation—about its importance. As an alternative, the information might suggest ways families can get involved (e.g., a flier on how to volunteer to read at story time when families find the library).

11. **Spotlight on Families.** Dedicate a bulletin board near the program's front lobby or office to spotlight the families of one class on a regular, rotating basis. Children in the chosen class can interview their families and create displays to feature on the bulletin board, including their families' responses during the interview, photographs, and drawings.

12. **Mystery Reader.** Each week, invite a family member to read aloud to the children during a time that works best for their schedule. To allow for the most flexibility, the family member could read in-person, live over a virtual video-conferencing platform, or via a prerecorded video. Engage children's curiosity and problem-solving skills by keeping the reader a mystery that the children have to solve. Before the mystery reader arrives (or, in the case of virtual participation, is visible on screen), provide children with three clues about the family member that are approved by that individual.

13. **Newsletters.** Send out newsletters regularly but keep them short and simple. Some useful information that you can feature includes

    - Classroom and/or program news and announcements

    - Recaps of events that recently took place

    - Reminders about upcoming events

    - A teacher or family member of the week

    - Suggested resources that tie into what's currently happening

    - A list of potential questions families might ask their teachers (to help prompt and encourage question asking)

Chapter 4: Meeting the Needs of Families Through Assessment

Key Chapter Points

1. Educators use assessments to get to know each child and to determine where a child is compared to "the learning progressions that children typically follow, including the typical sequences in which skills and concepts develop" (NAEYC 2020, 26). They also use assessments to reflect on and inform decisions and changes to curricular, instructional, and environmental practices in order to meet the developmental, individual, cultural, and linguistic needs of a child.

2. No matter what degree of experience families have with assessments, they have set goals and expectations for their children's development and growth, and they expect teachers and school leaders to facilitate these goals.

3. Educators should inform families about the assessments their children are required to take, when they will receive the results, and how to interpret the results. However, beyond these essentials, families have the right to more fully understand assessments.

4. The assessment team should consist of anyone who has an invested interest in the child: the child's family, the lead teacher, the instructional assistant, the school leader, the school counselor or psychologist, any specialists who work with the child, and sometimes an interpreter.

5. The assessment team forms at the start of the school year, when it sets goals, identifies strategies, and establishes timelines.

6. Families are critical team members within the Individualized Family Service Plan (IFSP) and Individualized Education Program (IEP) processes. An IFSP outlines the early intervention services provided to a young child and their family (Brillante 2017). An IEP lays out the special education instruction, supports, and services a child needs to thrive in the early learning program (Baumel 2022). However, many nondominant families feel isolated, alone, uneducated, anxious, and lost when they attend IEP meetings because of the jargon and terminology used (Peterson 2019; Reiman et al. 2010).

Strategies and Activities

1. **Family-Educator Conferences.** To help put families at ease during family-educator conferences, create a welcoming atmosphere. This includes providing comfortable seating, something to drink, materials to take notes during the conversation, and an agenda. During your discussion, create a document that captures the following information, with input from both educators and family members:

   - The child's strengths
   - The child's needs
   - Goals for the child
   - What is being worked on at the early learning program
   - Strategies being used at the early learning program
   - What is being worked on at home
   - Strategies being used at home
   - Action steps
   - Dates for check-in and follow-up

2. **Involve Children.** Before family-educator conferences, ask children to answer the following prompts:

   - My favorite thing to do at school is _____
   - I am working on learning how to _____

   Depending on their age, the child can write or draw their responses. They can also dictate their thinking behind what they write or draw for the teacher to transcribe. The child's perspective is important to have and to share with their family.

3. **Assessment Calendar.** Create a timeline, like the example shown in Table 5.4, that outlines when various types of assessments are scheduled and expected to occur. Share this calendar with families at the beginning of the school year.

Table 5.4. Assessment Calendar

Month	Step
August	Relationship building between the teacher and family to learn more about your child's strengths and interests
September	Assessment of learning domains
October	Assessment of content-area knowledge
November	Summative assessment
January	Assessment of interests and strengths, learning domains, and content-area knowledge
February	Summative assessment
March	Assessment of interests and strengths, learning domains, and content-area knowledge
May	Assessment of learning domains and content-area knowledge

4. **Family Feedback.** Throughout the school year, invite families to provide feedback about their child's learning experiences. You might send out a survey like the one in Table 5.5.

Table 5.5. Family Feedback Survey

My child's name is

The most important thing I need you to know about my child is

Rank the following statements about the experiences you and your child have had in the early learning program.

	True	Sometimes	Not True
My child is enjoying attending the program.	1	2	3
My child talks about friends they've made in the program.	1	2	3
My child talks about subjects, such as math, science, reading, and writing.	1	2	3
I feel welcomed in my child's classroom and in the larger early learning program.	1	2	3
I communicate often with my child's teacher.	1	2	3

Complete the next sections together with your child's teacher.

Collective Goals:

Action Steps:

Notes:

Keep It Going!

Educators receive a lot of information through these strategies and activities as well as through interactions with families. The next step is to analyze the information shared through outreach, dialogues, and questionnaires from families and to make the necessary changes to keep the partnership growing. The more the families see that their voices matter and elicit change, the more they will trust the process and partner with educators. A reciprocal family partnership is an ongoing process. It requires continuous evaluation and understanding of what is and isn't working. It also needs an occasional refresh. Keep the creativity flowing and get excited about the possibilities!

Teacher Feedback to School Leaders

It's important for school leaders to make sure things are working. A good practice is to regularly solicit feedback from staff regarding their needs related to family partnerships. Questionnaires like Table 5.6 are one way to start this process. School leaders can use the results from the questionnaire to schedule individual meetings, whole staff meetings, and professional development.

Table 5.6. Staff Questionnaire

Questions	Great	Okay	Terrible	Comment Explaining Why
How are you feeling in regards to connecting with the families in your classroom?				
How do you feel about the interactions you have had with the families in your classroom over the past few weeks?				
How do you feel I am doing as your school leader to facilitate connections and relationships with families?				

Family Feedback to Teachers and School Leaders

School leaders and teachers can survey families throughout the school year to gauge if their efforts are working and families are feeling positive. Consider the following questions for the survey:

1. Do you feel connected to your child's teacher? To the early learning program at large? If not, what would make you feel more connected?

2. Do you feel well-informed regarding what's happening at the early learning program? Regarding how your child is doing? If not, what could be improved?

3. Are there ample opportunities for you to share your feedback, ideas, and suggestions? Are there other ways you would like to share feedback?

Family Partnership Organizations for Educators and Families

Center for Applied Linguistics	www.cal.org	This nonprofit organization promotes language learning and cultural understanding, providing research, resources, and policy analysis.
Chalkbeat	www.chalkbeat.org	This nonprofit news organization covers efforts to improve schools for all children in the United States.
Child Trends	www.childtrends.org	This research organization focuses on improving the lives of children and youth, especially those who are most vulnerable.
Collaborative for Academic, Social, and Emotional Learning (CASEL)	www.casel.org	This nonprofit organization works to make evidence-based social and emotional learning an integral part of education from preschool through high school.
Council for Professional Recognition	www.cdacouncil.org	This professional organization works to ensure that all educators of children from birth to age 5 meet the developmental, emotional, and educational needs of the youngest children in the United States.
Division for Early Childhood (DEC) of the Council for Exceptional Children	www.dec-sped.org	This international organization promotes policies and advances evidence-based practices that support families and enhance the optimal development of children from birth to age 8 who have or are at risk for developmental delays and disabilities.
The Education Trust	www.edtrust.org	This research and advocacy organization focuses on advancing policies and practices to dismantle the racial and economic barriers embedded in the US education system.

EmbraceRace	www.embracerace.org	This nonprofit organization, started in 2016 by two parents, provides resources for families and educators of young children. It supports children's positive development of racial learning.
Families and Schools Together (FAST)	www.familiesandschools.org	This organization provides educators working with children of all ages training on and support for equity-focused family engagement best practices.
Families In Schools	www.familiesinschools.org	This advocacy organization involves families and communities in education to help their children succeed. It also provides educator trainings through professional development.
Family Diversity Projects	www.familydiversityprojects.org	This nonprofit organization works to eliminate prejudice, stereotyping, bullying, and harassment of people who are discriminated against due to sexual orientation, gender, gender identity, race, national origin, religion, and disabilities.
Family Engagement Lab	www.familyengagementlab.org	This national nonprofit offers family engagement tools for educators, consulting for professionals, and professional learning.
Family Resource Information, Education, and Network Development Service (FRIENDS) National Center for Community-Based Child Abuse Prevention	www.friendsnrc.org	This organization provides training and technical assistance to the community-based child abuse prevention agencies. Website resources available for families include education and support for fostering parental roles as experts and leaders.
Family Voices	www.familyvoices.org	This national family-led organization supports families and friends of children with special health care needs and disabilities.
Flamboyan Foundation	https://assess. flamboyanfoundation.org	This organization supports K–3 reading, arts revitalization, and family engagement. It provides early childhood educators with an assessment tool to gauge family engagement practices, give personalized recommendations, and suggest resources.
Global Family Research Project	www.globalfrp.org	The successor to the Harvard Family Research Project, this project works with policymakers, nonprofits, foundations, and educators to improve family engagement strategies to help families have a voice in their children's education.

GreatSchools	www.greatschools.org	This nonprofit organization provides data from state departments of education and the federal government. Families, researchers, and policymakers can find analysis, insights, and school quality ratings.
Learning Heroes	www.bealearninghero.org	This organization advances children's social, emotional, and academic development by providing free, research-based resources to help educators partner with families.
Mid-Atlantic Equity Consortium (MAEC)	www.maec.org	This nonprofit organization focuses on excellence and equity in education to achieve social justice. It provides family engagement resources via CAFE (Collaborative Action for Family Engagement), a federally funded regional statewide family engagement center in Maryland and Pennsylvania.
National Association for Bilingual Education (NABE)	www.nabe.org	This nonprofit membership organization advocates for educational equity and excellence for bilingual and multilingual children.
National Association for Family, School, and Community Engagement (NAFSCE)	www.nafsce.org	This membership association engages in policy work and provides programs and resources for professionals involved in family engagement.
The National Association for Multicultural Education (NAME)	www.nameorg.org	This nonprofit organization works to advance and advocate for social justice and educational equity through multicultural education. It provides free resources for professional development on culturally responsive teaching and other topics related to equitable education.
National Association for the Education of Young Children (NAEYC)	www.naeyc.org/our-work/for-families	NAEYC's "For Families" resources provide research-based tips and ideas for families on a variety of topics, including articles providing information about finding high-quality early childhood programs.
National Black Child Development Institute (NBCDI)	www.nbcdi.org	This national resource agency provides programs, publications, advocacy, and trainings related to early childhood care and education, health and wellness, literacy, and family engagement, primarily with Black children birth through age 8 and their families.

National Center for Families Learning (NCFL)	www.familieslearning.org	This organization promotes family education by engaging families, educators, administrators, and advocates to reduce education inequities. It provides resources and information on programming models, professional development, and community development.
National Education Association (NEA)	www.nea.org/student-success/engaged-families-communities/family-support	This organization provides resources for families, such as frequently asked questions about special education for multilingual families and family reading guides.
National PTA: The Center for Family Engagement	www.pta.org/the-center-for-family-engagement	This organization works with PTA leaders on family engagement through grants and other opportunities. It partners with other family engagement organizations with tools and resources for families to make positive changes and be a strong voice in their school communities to influence funding and practice decisions.
Parent Advocacy Coalition for Educational Rights (PACER) Center	www.pacer.org	This organization provides individual assistance, workshops, publications, and other resources to help families make decisions about education and other services for their children with disabilities.
Reaching At-Promise Students Association (RAPSA)	www.rapsa.org	This nonprofit membership organization helps educators working with at-risk children. Members include teachers, administrators, counselors, coaches, volunteers, and community members.
Scholastic Family and Community Engagement (FACE)	https://teacher.scholastic.com/products/face	This publisher program provides educators, families, and communities with the resources to boost the literacy skills of all children.
Teaching for Change	www.teachingforchange.org/educator-resources/parent-organizing	This organization provides resources for educators related to families and the concepts of racial equity, popular education, community organizing, and research on family engagement.
Understood	www.understood.org	This nonprofit organization provides resources and support for people with "learning and thinking differences," such as attention-deficit/hyperactivity disorder and dyslexia.
We Will All Rise	www.wewillallrise.org	This community-focused organization aims to create systematic change for young men of color via higher education, economic empowerment, and community engagement.

References

Alanís, I., & I.U. Iruka, eds. With S. Friedman. 2021. *Advancing Equity and Embracing Diversity in Early Childhood Education: Elevating Voices and Actions.* Washington, DC: NAEYC.

Allen, R., D.L. Shapland, J. Neitzel, & I.U. Iruka. 2021. "Creating Anti-Racist Early Childhood Spaces." Viewpoint. *Young Children* 76 (2): 49–54.

Aratani, Y., V.R. Wight, & J.L. Cooper. 2011. *Racial Gaps in Early Childhood: Socio-Emotional Health, Developmental, and Educational Outcomes Among African-American Boys.* Report. New York: National Center for Children in Poverty. www.nccp.org/publication/racial-gaps-in-early-childhood.

Banks, J.A., & C.A. McGee Banks, eds. 2005. *Multicultural Education: Issues and Perspectives.* 5th ed. Hoboken, NJ: John Wiley & Sons.

Barger, M.M., E.M. Kim, N.R. Kuncel, & E.M. Pomerantz. 2019. "The Relation Between Parents' Involvement in Children's Schooling and Children's Adjustment: A Meta-Analysis." *Psychological Bulletin Journal* 145 (9): 855–90.

Barrera, I., & R.M. Corso. 2002. "Cultural Competency as Skilled Dialogue." *Topics in Early Childhood Special Education* 22 (2): 103–13.

Barton, A.C., C. Drake, J.G. Perez, K.S. Louis, & M. George. 2004. "Ecologies of Parental Engagement in Urban Education." *Educational Researcher* 33 (4): 3–12.

Bassett, L. With A. Devercelli, S.L. Mottee, I.P.L. Giroux, & E. Humphry. 2018. "Early Stimulation: Supporting Parents to Help Their Children Thrive." *Guidance Note,* September. Washington, DC: Early Learning Partnership, World Bank. https://documents1.worldbank.org/curated/en/805721544007101483/pdf/Early-Stimulation-Supporting-Parents-to-Help-Their-Children-Thrive.pdf.

Baumel, J. 2022. "What Is an IEP?" *GreatSchools,* last updated October 26. www.greatschools.org/gk/articles/what-is-an-iep.

Belsky, G. n.d. "What Is an IEP?" *Understood for All.* Accessed January 31, 2022. www.understood.org/en/articles/what-is-an-iep.

Berns, R.M. 2004. *Child, Family, School, Community: Socialization and Support.* 6th ed. Belmont, CA: Wadsworth/Thomson Learning.

Bloom, P.J., & M.B. Abel. 2015. "Expanding the Lens—Leadership as an Organizational Asset." *Young Children* 70 (2): 10–17.

Bodrova, E., & D.J. Leong. 2018. "Common Assessment Terms and How to Use Them: A Glossary for Early Childhood Educators." In *Spotlight on Young Children: Observation and Assessment,* eds. H. Bohart & R. Procopio, 15–20. Washington, DC: NAEYC.

Brillante, P. 2017. *The Essentials: Supporting Young Children with Disabilities in the Classroom.* Washington, DC: NAEYC.

Bronfenbrenner, U. 1979. *The Ecology of Human Development: Experiments by Nature and Design.* Cambridge, MA: Harvard University Press.

Bronfenbrenner, U. 1989. "Ecological Systems Theory." *Annals of Child Development* 6 (1): 187–249.

Bronfenbrenner, U., ed. 2005. *Making Human Beings Human: Bioecological Perspectives on Human Development.* Thousand Oaks, CA: SAGE Publications.

Bryan, J., & L. Henry. 2008. "Strengths-Based Partnerships: A School-Family-Community Partnership Approach to Empowering Students." *Professional School Counseling* 12 (2): 149–56.

Bullard, J. 2017. *Creating Environments for Learning: Birth to Age Eight.* 3rd ed. New York: Pearson.

Camera, L. 2021. "Study Confirms School-to-Prison Pipeline." *US News and World Report,* July 27. www.usnews.com/news/education-news/articles/2021-07-27/study-confirms-school-to-prison-pipeline.

Carter, P.L. 2005. *Keepin' It Real: School Success Beyond Black and White.* New York: Oxford University Press.

CAST (Center for Applied Special Technology). 2020. "UDL Tips for Assessments." Wakefield, MA: CAST. www.cast.org/products-services/resources/2020/udl-tips-assessments.

Catalino, T., & L.E. Meyer, eds. 2016. *Environment: Promoting Meaningful Access, Participation, and Inclusion.* DEC Recommended Practices Monograph Series No. 2. Washington, DC: Division for Early Childhood.

Charania, M.R. 2021. *Family Engagement Reimagined: Innovations Strengthening Family-School Connections to Help Students Thrive.* Lexington, MA: Christensen Institute. www.christenseninstitute.org/wp-content/uploads/2021/09/Families-9.28.pdf.

Chen, J-Q., & G.D. McNamee. 2007. *Bridging: Assessment for Teaching and Learning in Early Childhood Classrooms, PreK–3.* Thousand Oaks, CA: Corwin Press.

Childre, A., & C.R. Chambers. 2005. "Family Perceptions of Student-Centered Planning and IEP Meetings." *Education and Training in Developmental Disabilities* 40 (3): 217–33.

Clark, R.M. 1983. *Family Life and School Achievement: Why Poor Black Children Succeed or Fail.* Chicago: The University of Chicago Press.

Conchas, G.Q. 2006. *The Color of Success: Race and High-Achieving Urban Youth.* New York: Teachers College Press.

Cork, L. 2005. *Supporting Black Pupils and Parents: Understanding and Improving Home–School Relations.* New York: Routledge.

DEC (Division for Early Childhood of the Council for Exceptional Young Children). 2014. *DEC Recommended Practices in Early Intervention/Early Childhood Special Education.* Missoula, MT: DEC. www.dec-sped.org/recommendedpractices.

DEC (Division for Early Childhood of the Council for Exceptional Young Children). 2020. *Initial Practice-Based Standards for Early Interventionists/Early Childhood Special Educators.* Missoula, MT: DEC. www.dec-sped.org/ei-ecse-standards.

DeHaney, F.L., C.T. Payton, & A. Washington. 2021. "Quality Includes Removing Bias from Early Childhood Education Environments." *Young Children* 76 (2): 12–20.

Delpit, L. 2006. *Other People's Children: Cultural Conflict in the Classroom.* New York: The New Press.

Derman-Sparks, L., & J.O. Edwards. With C.M. Goins. 2020. *Anti-Bias Education for Young Children and Ourselves.* 2nd ed. Washington, DC: NAEYC.

Elicker, J., & M. McMullen. 2013. "Appropriate and Meaningful Assessment in Family-Centered Programs." *Young Children* 68 (3): 22–26.

Epstein, J.L., M.G. Sanders, S.B. Sheldon, B.S. Simon, K.C. Salinas, N.R. Jansorn, F.L. Van Voorhis, C.S. Martin, B.G. Thomas, M.D. Greenfeld, D.J. Hutchins, & K.J. Williams. 2019. *School, Family, and Community Partnerships: Your Handbook for Action.* 4th ed. Thousand Oaks, CA: Corwin.

Epstein, J.L., & S.B. Sheldon. 2006. "Moving Forward: Ideas for Research on School, Family, and Community Partnerships." In *The SAGE Handbook for Research in Education: Engaging Ideas and Enriching Inquiry,* eds. C.F. Conrad & R.C. Serlin, 117–38. Thousand Oaks, CA: SAGE Publications.

Erdman, S., & L.J. Colker. With E.C. Winter. 2020. *Trauma and Young Children: Teaching Strategies to Support and Empower.* Washington, DC: NAEYC.

Eriksson, M., M. Ghazinour, & A. Hammarstrom. 2018. "Different Uses of Bronfenbrenner's Ecological Theory in Public Mental Health Research: What Is Their Value for Guiding Public Mental Health Policy and Practice?" *Social Theory and Health* 16 (4): 414–33.

Fashola, O.S., ed. 2005. *Educating African American Males: Voices from the Field.* Thousand Oaks, CA: Corwin Press.

Fenton, A., K. Walsh, S. Wong, & T. Cumming. 2014. "Using Strengths-Based Approaches in Early Years Practice and Research." *International Journal of Early Childhood* 47 (1): 27–52.

Ferlazzo, L. 2011. "Involvement or Engagement?" *Educational Leadership* 68 (8): 10–14.

Fields, M.V., P. Meritt, & D.M. Fields. 2018. *Constructive Guidance and Discipline: Birth to Age Eight.* 7th ed. New York: Pearson.

Fritzgerald, A. 2021. "Honor as Power: The Practical Keys to Antiracist Teaching." *ASCD Express* 16 (14). www.ascd.org/el/articles/honor-as-power-the-practical-keys-to-antiracist-teaching.

Gestwicki, C. 2017. *Developmentally Appropriate Practice: Curriculum and Development in Early Education.* 6th ed. Boston: Cengage.

Gillanders, C., I.U. Iruka, C. Bagwell, & T. Adejumo. 2021. "Parents' Perceptions of a K–3 Formative Assessment." *School Community Journal* 31 (2): 239–66.

Gonzalez-Mena, J. 2007. *50 Early Childhood Strategies for Working and Communicating with Diverse Families.* New York: Pearson.

Gonzalez-Mena, J. 2012. *Child, Family, and Community: Family-Centered Early Care and Education.* 6th ed. New York: Pearson.

Granata, K. 2014. "Welcoming Family Diversity in the Classroom." *Education World.* www.educationworld.com/a_curr/welcoming-diverse-family-structures.shtml.

Grant, K.B., & J.A. Ray. 2016. *Home, School, and Community Collaboration: Culturally Responsive Family Engagement.* 3rd ed. Thousand Oaks, CA: SAGE Publications.

Gray, C., & S. MacBlain. 2015. *Learning Theories in Childhood.* 2nd ed. Thousand Oaks, CA: SAGE Publications.

Graybill, O., & L.B. Easton. 2015. "The Art of Dialogue." *Educational Leadership* 72 (7). Online Exclusive. www.ascd.org/el/articles/the-art-of-dialogue.

Hammond, Z. 2015. *Culturally Responsive Teaching and the Brain: Promoting Authentic Engagement and Rigor Among Culturally and Linguistically Diverse Students.* Thousand Oaks, CA: Corwin.

Hayes, N., L. O'Toole, & A.M. Halpenny. 2017. *Introducing Bronfenbrenner: A Guide for Practitioners and Students in Early Years Education.* London: Routledge.

Hedges, H., J. Cullen, & B. Jordan. 2011. Early Years Curriculum: Funds of Knowledge as a Conceptual Framework for Children's Interests. *Curriculum Studies* 43 (2): 185–205.

Henderson, A., K. Mapp, V. Johnson, & D. Davies. 2007. *Beyond the Bake Sale: The Essential Guide to Family-School Partnerships.* New York: New Press.

Hill, C.F., J.R. Newton, & M.C. Williams. 2017. "Check Your Judgment: Reframing Techniques to Support Strengths-Based Approaches to Family-Centered Practices." In *Family: Knowing Families, Tailoring Practices, Building Capacity* (DEC Recommended Practices Monograph Series No. 3), eds. C.M. Trivette & B. Keilty, 1–8. Arlington, VA: Division for Early Childhood.

Hing, J. 2014. "Black Students Most Underrepresented Among AP Test Takers." *Colorlines,* February 13. https://colorlines.com/article/black-students-most-underrepresented-among-ap-test-takers.

Ishimaru, A.M. 2020. *Just Schools: Building Equitable Collaborations with Families and Communities*. New York: Teachers College Press.

Joseph, M. 2022. "School Culture Vs. School Climate: The Two Are Not Synonymous." *District Administration,* November 4. https://districtadministration.com/school-culture-vs-school-climate-the-two-are-not-synonymous.

Jung, S.B., & S. Sheldon. 2020. "Connecting Dimensions of School Leadership for Partnerships with School and Teacher Practices of Family Engagement." *School Community Journal* 30 (1): 9–32.

Karpov, Y.V. 2014. *Vygotsky for Educators*. New York: Cambridge University Press.

King-Hill, S. 2015. "Critical Analysis of Maslow's Hierarchy of Needs." *The STeP Journal* 2 (4): 54–57.

Knight, J. 2022. "Friendship, Culture, and Parenting: Using Case Study Data to Reflect on Home Visiting Practices." Voices of Practitioners. *Young Children* 77 (4): 68–74.

Knowlton, E., & D. Mulanax. 2001. "Education Programs for Parents and Families of Children and Youth with Developmental Disabilities." In *Handbook of Diversity in Parent Education: The Changing Faces of Parenting and Parent Education,* eds. M.J. Fine & S.W. Lee, 299–314. San Diego: Academic Press.

Kohl, H. 1994. *"I Won't Learn from You": And Other Thoughts on Creative Maladjustment.* New York: The New Press.

Koralek, D., K. Nemeth, & K. Ramsey. 2019. *Families and Educators Together: Building Great Relationships that Support Young Children*. Washington, DC: NAEYC.

Kostelnik, M.J., A.K. Soderman, A.P. Whiren, & M. Rupiper. 2019. *Developmentally Appropriate Curriculum: Best Practices in Early Childhood Education*. 7th ed. New York: Pearson.

Kuru Cetin, S., & P. Taskin. 2016. "Parent Involvement in Education in Terms of their Socio-Economic Status." *Eurasian Journal of Educational Research* 2016 (66): 105–22.

Lim, L., & P. Renshaw. 2001. "The Relevance of Sociocultural Theory to Culturally Diverse Partnerships and Communities." *Journal of Child and Family Studies* 10 (1): 9–21.

Lin, M., & A. Bates. 2010. "Home Visits: How Do They Affect Teachers' Beliefs About Teaching and Diversity?" *Early Childhood Education Journal* 38 (3): 179–85.

Lipsitz, J., & T. West. 2006. "What Makes a Good School? Identifying Excellent Middle Schools." *Phi Delta Kappan* 88 (1): 57–66.

Lowenhaupt, R. 2014. "School Access and Participation: Family Engagement Practices in the New Latino Diaspora." *Education and Urban Society* 46 (5): 522–47.

Maguire, P. 1987. *Doing Participatory Research: A Feminist Approach*. Amherst, MA: The Center for International Education, School of Education, University of Massachusetts.

Mammen, S., Y. Sano, B. Braun, & E.F. Maring. 2019. "Shaping Core Health Messages: Rural, Low-Income Mothers Speak Through Participatory Action Research." *Health Communication* 34 (10): 1141–9.

Mapp, K.L., & E. Bergman. 2021. *Embracing a New Normal: Toward a More Liberatory Approach to Family Engagement*. Report. New York: Carnegie Corporation of New York. https://media.carnegie.org/filer_public/f6/04/f604e672-1d4b-4dc3-903d-3b619a00cd01/fe_report_fin.pdf.

Maslow, A.H. 1954. *Motivation and Personality*. New York: Harper.

McLeod, N. 2020. "Towards an Understanding of 'School' Readiness: Collective Interpretations and Priorities." *Educational Action Research* 28 (5): 723–41.

Meeker, E. 2015. "Using Trauma-Sensitive Strategies to Support Family Engagement and Effective Collaboration, Transcript." Webinar. CADRE, December 3. www.cadreworks.org/resources/cadre-materials/using-trauma-sensitive-strategies-support-family-engagement-and-effective.

Mellott, A. 2021. "Tearing Down Silos: A Model for Interagency Collaboration." *Young Children* 76 (4): 38–44.

Moll, L., C. Amanti, D. Neff, & N. Gonzales. 1992. "Funds of Knowledge for Teaching: Using a Qualitative Approach to Connect Homes and Classrooms." *Theory into Practice* 31 (2): 132–41.

Mueller, T.G., & P.C. Buckley. 2014. "The Odd Man Out: How Father Navigate the Special Education System." *Remedial and Special Education* 35 (1): 40–49.

NAEYC. 2016. *Code of Ethical Conduct and Statement of Commitment*. Brochure. Rev. ed. Washington, DC: NAEYC.

NAEYC. 2019. "Advancing Equity in Early Childhood Education." Position statement. Washington, DC: NAEYC. www.naeyc.org/resources/position-statements/equity.

NAEYC. 2020. "Developmentally Appropriate Practice." Position statement. Washington, DC: NAEYC. www.naeyc.org/resources/position-statements/dap.

NAEYC. 2021. *Ensuring Quality Early Childhood Education Professional Preparation Programs: NAEYC's Early Childhood Higher Education Accreditation Standards*. Washington, DC: NAEYC. www.naeyc.org/accreditation/higher-ed/standards.

NAEYC. 2022. *Developmentally Appropriate Practice in Early Childhood Programs Serving Children from Birth Through Age 8*. 4th ed. Washington, DC: NAEYC.

NAFSCE (National Association for Family, School, and Community Engagement). 2022. *Family Engagement Core Competencies: A Body of Knowledge, Skills, and Dispositions for Family-Facing Professionals*. Alexandria, VA: NAFSCE.

NASEM (National Academies of Sciences, Engineering, and Medicine). 2016. *Parenting Matters: Supporting Parents of Children Ages 0–8*. Report. Washington, DC: The National Academies Press.

National Council for the Social Studies. 2010. *National Curriculum Standards for Social Studies: A Framework for Teaching, Learning, and Assessment*. Silver Spring, MD: National Council for the Social Studies.

NCTSN (The National Child Traumatic Stress Network). n.d. "Populations at Risk." Accessed January 18, 2023. www.nctsn.org/what-is-child-trauma/populations-at-risk.

Nelson, J., & L. Brooks. 2015. *Racial Equity Toolkit: An Opportunity to Operationalize Equity*. Berkeley, CA: Government Alliance on Race and Equity. https://racialequityalliance.org/wp-content/uploads/2015/10/GARE-Racial_Equity_Toolkit.pdf.

Nieto, S. 2004. *Affirming Diversity: The Sociopolitical Context of Multicultural Education*. 4th ed. New York: Allyn & Bacon.

Noltemeyer, A., A. James, K. Bush, D. Bergen, V. Barrios, & J. Patton. 2021. "The Relationship Between Deficiency Needs and Growth Needs: The Continuing Investigation of Maslow's Theory." *Child and Youth Services* 42 (1): 24–42.

Othering and Belonging Institute. n.d. "Bridging and Belonging." Accessed January 26, 2023. https://belonging.berkeley.edu/bridging-belonging.

Park, P., M. Brydon-Miller, B. Hall, & T. Jackson. 1993. *Voices of Change: Participatory Research in the United States and Canada.* Westport, CT: Bergin & Garvey.

Peterson, J. 2019. "Taking Parent Fear and Anxiety Out of the Evaluation and IEP Process." *RethinkEd,* June 11. www.rethinked.com/resources/taking-parent-fear-and-anxiety-out-of-the-evaluation-and-iep-process.

Proctor, D. 2021. "New Narratives of Hope This Black History Month–And Beyond." *Robert Wood Johnson Foundation's Culture of Health Blog,* February 9. www.rwjf.org/en/blog/2018/02/new-narratives-of-hope-this-black-history-month.html.

Rashid, H. 2009. "From Brilliant Baby to Child Placed at Risk: The Perilous Path of African American Boys in Early Childhood Education." *Journal of Negro Education* 78 (3): 347–55.

Reiman, J.W., L. Beck, T. Coppola, & A. Engiles. 2010. *Parents' Experiences with the IEP Process Considerations for Improving Practice.* Literature review. Eugene, OR: Center for Appropriate Dispute Resolution in Special Education. www.cadreworks.org/resources/literature-article/parents-experiences-iep-process-considerations-improving-practice.

Rosa, E.M., & J.R.H. Tudge. 2013. "Urie Bronfenbrenner's Theory of Human Development: Its Evolution from Ecology to Bioecology." *Journal of Family Theory and Review* 5 (6): 243–58.

Rosales, J., & T. Walker. 2021. "The Racist Beginnings of Standardized Testing." *National Education Association,* March 20. www.nea.org/advocating-for-change/new-from-nea/racist-beginnings-standardized-testing.

Sabol, T.J., C.L. Kessler, L.O. Rogers, A. Petitclerc, J. Silver. M. Briggs-Gowan, & L.S. Wakschlag. 2021. "A Window into Racial and Socioeconomic Status Disparities in Preschool Disciplinary Action Using Developmental Methodology." *Annals of the New York Academy of Sciences* 1508 (1): 123–36.

Saint-Jacques, M., D. Turcotte, & E. Pouliot. 2009. "Adopting a Strengths Perspective in Social Work Practice with Families in Difficulty: From Theory to Practice." *Families in Society* 90 (4): 454–61.

Shelton, L.G. 2019. *The Bronfenbrenner Primer: A Guide to Dexlecology.* New York: Routledge.

Sheridan, S.M., & E.M. Kim, eds. 2015. *Foundational Aspects of Family-School Partnership Research.* New York: Springer.

Sheridan, S.M., N. Koziol, A.L. Witte, I. Iruka, & L.L. Knoche. 2020. "Longitudinal and Geographic Trends in Family Engagement During the Pre-Kindergarten to Kindergarten Transition." *Early Childhood Education Journal* 48: 365–77.

Silloway, T., & J. Szrom. 2022. *Strengthening Families with Infants and Toddlers: A Policy Framework for States.* Report. Washington, DC: National Infant-Toddler Court Program, ZERO TO THREE. www.zerotothree.org/resource/strengthening-families-with-infants-and-toddlers-a-policy-framework-for-states.

Smith, T.E., W.M. Reinke, K.C. Herman, & F. Huang. 2019. "Understanding Family–School Engagement Across and Within Elementary- and Middle-School Contexts." *School Psychology* 34 (4): 363–75.

Soule, N. 2020. "'I Know That Maybe I Need to Be a Little More Kind': Three Methods to Build Educator Empathy and Capacity for Family Engagement." *Promising Practices in Pre-Service Educator Preparation* (blog), December 17. https://nafsce.org/page/Threemethods.

Staake, J. 2018. "Using a House System in the Classroom." *WeAreTeachers,* July 3. www.weareteachers.com/house-system-in-schools.

Trivette, C.M., & B. Keilty, eds. 2017. *Family: Knowing Families, Tailoring Practices, Building Capacity*. DEC Recommended Practices Monograph Series No. 3. Arlington, VA: Division for Early Childhood.

Tschannen-Moran, M., & W.K. Hoy. 2000. "A Multidisciplinary Analysis of the Nature, Meaning, and Measurement of Trust." *Review of Educational Research* 70 (4): 547–93.

Veugelers, W. 2017. "The Moral in Paulo Freire's Educational Work: What Moral Education Can Learn from Paulo Freire." *Journal of Moral Education* 46 (4): 412–21.

Weiss, H.B., S.M. Bouffard, B.L. Bridglall, & E.W. Gordon. 2009. *Reframing Family Involvement in Education: Supporting Families to Support Educational Equity.* Equity Matters: Research Review No. 5. New York: The Campaign for Educational Equity. www.tc.columbia.edu/i/a/document/12018_EquityMattersVol5_Web.pdf.

Williams, J. 2019. *Teach Boldly: Using Edtech for Social Good*. Portland, OR: International Society for Technology in Education.

Wink, J. 2005. *Critical Pedagogy: Notes from the Real World*. 3rd ed. Boston: Pearson.

Yamauchi, L.A., E. Ponte, K.T. Ratliffe, & K. Traynor. 2017. "Theoretical and Conceptual Frameworks Used in Research on Family-School Partnerships." *School Community Journal* 27 (2): 9–34.

Index

Page numbers followed by *f* and *t* indicate figures and tables, respectively.